NO FRILLS Exam Prep Books

Intellectual Properties, Trademarks and Copyrights

Contents of this book are fully copyrighted. We develop study material entirely on our own. Braindump is strictly prohibited. We provide essential knowledge contents, NOT any generalized "study system" kind of "pick-the-right-answer-every time" techniques or "visit this link" referrals.

Contents Update

All books come with LIFE TIME FREE UPDATES. When you find a newer version of the purchased book all you need to do is to go and download. **Please check our web site's Free Updates section regularly:**

http://www.examreview.net/free_updates.htm

Page Formatting and Typeface

To accommodate the needs of those with weaker vision, we use LARGER PRINT throughout the book whenever practical. The text in this book was created using Garamond (size 16). A little bit of page resizing, however, may have happened along the actual book printing process.

The Exams

The Microsoft Technology Associate MTA certification is an entry-level certification which serves as a good starting point for students and educators who may eventually progress to the higher programs. Simply put, it assesses the foundational knowledge necessary to pursue MCSE, MCSD and the like.

12 16

The MTA certification focuses more on knowledge and a little less on skills. However, the knowledge areas are all based on MS products so you must know those products inside and out. Questions on the general knowledge are relatively easy. Product and technology specific technical questions, however, are way more difficult. This is why we developed this study product - we focus on those difficult topics that involve difficult technical skills. We want you to be able to answer these difficult questions and secure exam success accordingly. Exam 98-366: Networking Fundamentals deals with the basics of Windows networking. Exam 98-367: Security Fundamentals is designed to provide candidates with an assessment of their knowledge of fundamental security concepts. Both exams share many common knowledge topics so it makes sense to study both together.

We give you knowledge information relevant to the exam specifications. To be able to succeed in the real exams, you'll need to apply your earned knowledge to the question scenarios. **To succeed in the exams, you need to read as many reference books as possible. There is no single book that can cover everything!**

You should also download the evaluation copy of Windows Server 2008 R2 and play with it. You can use it for free for max 240 days. You should download the ISO image file and burn a DVD disc out of it, then perform installation accordingly.

Although there is a **VHD** version available, we do not recommend that you use it for testing. There are some complicated steps involved which may not always go as smooth.

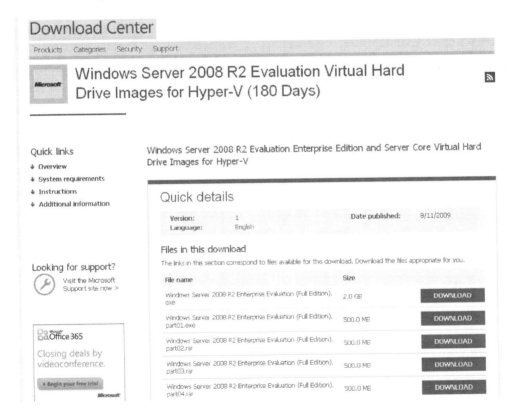

Table of Contents (MTA Exams)

Windows based Networking & Security Features

Overview

A computer network is a system for communication between individual computers. These networks may be fixed via cabling or temporary via modems or other remote connection methods. A server is a computer on a network that manages network resources. A file server is a computer and storage device dedicated to storing files. A print server is a computer that manages one or more printers. A network server is a computer that manages network traffic. A database server is a computer system that processes database queries.

Servers are mostly dedicated, that they would perform no other tasks besides their assigned server tasks. You do not do your work on the server. You do your work on your own desktop PC, then save your works on the server. The basic components of a server and a regular PC are the same. The two primarily differ in these aspects:

● Intended use	● Number of processors
● Workload	● Amount of RAM
● Physical storage	● Specialized storage
	● Maintenance

High-end servers perform very specific jobs, and that their designs always require fault-free operation - the server is not expected to crash at all.

Server roles

The minimum specification for a server hardware would depend largely on the role the server is going to play, the processes and services that will run on it, and the number of users it will have. Also note that a server can be configured to perform specific roles. The applications that the server runs determine the particular server's role. For a server to undertake a role, additional services and features will have to be installed. This is why the server's role is the single most important factor in determining the hardware that a server requires. Typical server roles include:

- Backup server

- Database server

- Domain controller

- Directory Server

- File server

- Print server

- RAS server

- Web server

- Email server

Do note that in the world of Windows computing, a domain controller stores a copy of Active Directory and maintains the directory data store. Active Directory aims to provide a centralized repository of information for securely managing an organization's resources.

An operating system is the most important program that runs on a computer. Every computer must have an operating system to run other programs. It performs all the basic tasks, such as recognizing input from the keyboard, sending output to the display screen, keeping track of files and directories on the disk, and controlling peripheral devices of all kinds. Server operating system differs from a desktop one in that it is often optimized for handling processes that run behind the scenes (the background processes).

Virtualization

With Virtualization technologies a single physical device can act like having multiple physical versions of itself for sharing across the network. This is usually done with the help of multiple processor cores in the same processor die. Platform virtualization is performed by the host software. As a control program, this host creates a simulated computer environment for formulating a virtual machine to serve the guest software. With full virtualization, the virtual machine will simulate sufficient hardware functionality to allow an unmodified OS to run in isolation. On the other hand, with paravirtualization the virtual machine will not simulate hardware but will simply offer a special API to serve those modified guest OS.

Hyper-V is a server role that provides tools and services one can use to create a virtualized server computing environment. This feature requires an x64-based processor, hardware-assisted virtualization, and hardware data execution prevention DEP. You add this role via Server Manager - Add Roles. You create a new virtual machine via Administrative Tools - Hyper-V Manager.

You can also create virtual networks on the server running Hyper-V for use with the various virtual machines and virtualization server. An external network provides communication between a virtual machine and a physical network. An internal network provides communication between the virtualization server and virtual machines. A private network provides communication between virtual machines. All these can be configured via the Hyper-V Manager -> Virtual Network Manager.

Cloud Computing

Cloud computing is all about distributed computing. An application is built using resources from multiple services from the same or different locations. By knowing the endpoint to access the services, the user can use software as a service, much like utility computing. Behind the scene there are grids of computers and the user does not need to know the details of the background stuff.

Grid computing describes the act of sharing tasks over multiple computers. A computational grid works by applying the resources of multiple computers together to resolving a single problem. A private cloud is a cloud computing infrastructure operated solely for a single organization. **In any case, cloud computing is energy friendly because people are effectively sharing computing resources.**

Load balancing

One way to achieve server scalability is to have more servers added to the configuration so to distribute the load among the group of servers (server cluster). The load distribution among these servers is what we call load balancing. When there are multiple servers in a server group, network traffic needs to be evenly distributed among the servers.

Round Robin Load Balancing is primarily for DNS service. There is a built-in round robin feature of the BIND DNS server. It works by cycling through the IP addresses corresponding to a server group. Hardware load balancers are dedicated for routing TCP/IP packets to various servers in a cluster. They are more efficient and way costlier. Software Load Balancers are usually options that come shipped with expensive server application packages. Software based solutions usually cost less but are often application specific.

Network Infrastructure and Basic Windows Networking

A typical top down approach to network infrastructure design requires that you understand the constraints and objectives of network use as well as the applications and data on which your business relies upon on, before considering the viable tech options. It is therefore advisable that you start with the business objectives because your network has the most important mission of helping end users in achieving their business objectives.

Server Message Block SMB is the protocol deployed by Windows for file sharing and other communications. It serves as the basis for NetBIOS communications and resources sharing over the network. SMB traffic stays in LAN only.

Share permissions apply only when a user is accessing a file or folder non-locally. They can be applied on a user or on a group level, although assigning permissions on a group basis is always recommended. Individual permissions and group permissions can be combined to form the user's effective permissions. NTFS permissions allow you to assign permissions more granularly at the folder and file level while Share permissions are limited to the folder level only. Keep in mind, file permissions always take precedence over folder permissions.

Event Viewer is the interface for managing event logging in Windows. The primary types of log are System logs, Application logs and Security logs. It is always advised that you focus on monitoring failed login/access attempts.

Single sign-on SSO refers to the kind of access control method which enables a user to authenticate once and gain access to network resources of other software systems. Kerberos is an authentication protocol in use by the newer Windows Servers (since Windows 2000) for facilitating the implementation of SSO.

SNMP is deployed by many network management systems for monitoring network-attached devices for conditions that warrant administrative attention. The SNMP protocol itself does not define which information a managed system should offer. Instead, it relies on the various management information bases MIBs to do the job. The Microsoft SMS System Management Server makes extensive use of SNMP. The community string serves as kind of a "password" for SNMP communication. Do note that the use of SNMP will increase network load quite a bit.

On a Windows network with Active Directory enabled, information necessary for authentication is stored in the directory – that is, each Domain Controller holds a copy – information is replicated across the entire network domain. If you have multiple domain controllers up and running, server failure would not disrupt authentication unless all domain controllers within a domain fail altogether.

Open System Interconnect

It offers a 7 layer model which can be used as a guideline for systematic network design, management and troubleshooting.

- The Application Layer is responsible for identifying and establishing the availability of desired communication partner and verifying sufficient resources exist for communication.

- The Presentation Layer is responsible for presenting the data in standard formats and provides services such as data compression, decompression, encryption, and decryption.

- The Session Layer is responsible for coordinating communication between network nodes.

- The Transport Layer is responsible for flow control, with the primary aim of maintaining data integrity. Simply put, it works to ensure complete data transfer.

- The Network Layer has the primary responsibility of sending data packets from the source network to the destination network using a pre-specified routing method.

- The Data Link Layer is divided into the sub-layers of Logical Link Control (LLC) and Media Access Control (MAC). The LLC sub-layer handles tasks such as error control, flow control and framing, while the MAC sub-layer handles access to shared media.

- The Physical Layer allows the actual flow of signals.

- Routing takes place at layer 3. On the other hand, switching takes place at layer 2. Routing requires more complicated configuration (usually).

Routing and switching

TCP/IP is the communication language of internet networking devices. It requires routing in order to reach the outside networks. In other words, you need to use router to connect different networks together. Routing table is the major element required for making routing decision by the routers. Main considerations while building this routing table may include Administrative distance and Metrics amidst others.

Routing protocols are for routers to communicate with each others. Routing Information Protocol RIP is an example of routing protocol. It is a distance-vector routing protocol which uses information provided to it by its neighboring routers to maintain information in a routing table on the cost of routing entries, measured in the units of hops and other metrics. A routed protocol contains the actual data elements. It can be routed by a router. TCP/IP itself is a routed protocol.

RIP for dynamic routing configuration is easy to setup but offers poor scalability as it's mechanism is limited by hop counts (the route with the fewest number of hops is always the best route), thus is mostly for LAN use. OSPF is better for large network due to a more sophisticated mechanism (it determines the best route by taking into account bandwidth as well as other factors) but is more complicated to set up. BGP is strictly a routing protocol for WAN.

Technically a Windows Server is acting as a router if it has multiple network interfaces connecting to different network segments. It supports routing protocols such as RIP (version 2).

IP Addressing

To build and run a large network, you will have to take care of IP addresses subnet configuration and possibly routing table configuration.

You may as well want to deploy routing protocols. This holds true for both LAN and WAN.

An IP address is the unique number ID assigned to one network interface. It is 32 bit based (as per IPv4).A subnet is a portion of a network sharing a particular subnet address. The gateway address is the router's address. In a Class A address, the first octet is the network portion. In a Class B address, the first two octets are the network portion. In a Class C address, the first three octets are the network portion. Multicast IP addresses are Class D IP addresses ranging from 224.0.0.0 to 239.255.255.255.

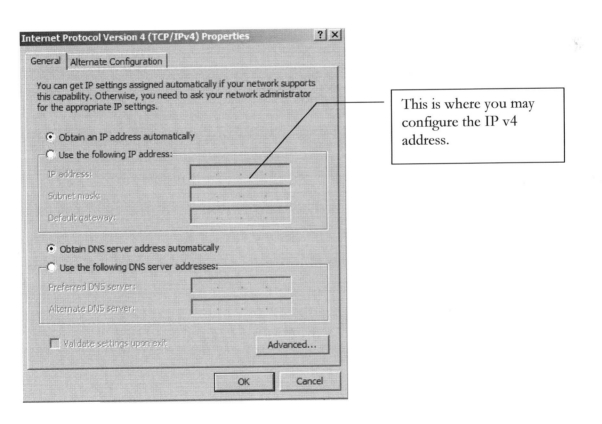

This is where you may configure the IP v4 address.

You want to know the address ranges:

IP V4 Address Classes	Leftmost bits	Start range	End range
A	0xxx	0.0.0.0	127.255.255.255
B	10xx	128.0.0.0	191.255.255.255
C	110x	192.0.0.0	223.255.255.255
D	1110	224.0.0.0	239.255.255.255
E	1111	240.0.0.0	255.255.255.255

Class D addresses are for multicast, while class E addresses are reserved. 255.255.255.255 is a limited broadcast address. 127.0.0.1 is the loopback address for testing purpose. Also note that these are the private address ranges (for use internally without capabilities of internet access):

V4 Classes	Private start range	Private end range
A	10.0.0.0	10.255.255.255
B	172.16.0.0	172.31.255.255
C	192.168.0.0	192.168.255.255

Private IP addresses are non-routable and are strictly for private use inside a private network. Many hosts can automatically configure their IP settings to use private addresses.

The IPv6 address space has 128 bits, which is broken down into eight groups of 16 bits. There are two major 64-bit parts, which are the network prefix (contains the registry, provider, subscriber ID, and subnet) that occupies the higher order groups of bits and the interface ID that occupies the lower bits.

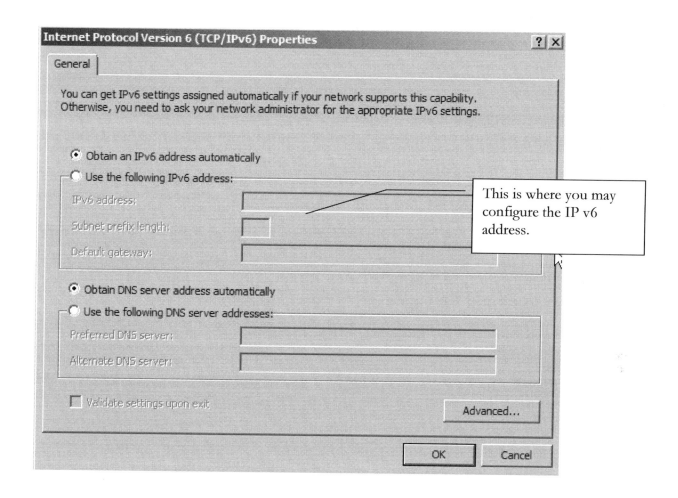

Server 2008 R2 supports both IPV4 and IPV6 addressing natively.

IP subnetting

A subnet mask has four bytes thus totaling 32 bits. It is often written using the dotted-decimal notation, with the leftmost bits always set to the value of 1. Network hosts on different subnets are only allowed to communicate through routers (regular switches won't do the tricks). By applying a subnet mask to an IP address you effectively split the address into two parts, the first being an extended network address and the second being a host address.

Classless Interdomain Routing CLDR improves both address space utilization and routing scalability by having an IP network represented by a prefix. It is not yet the mainstream in most small to mid size environments though. On the other hand, Variable Length Subnet Masks (VLSM) allows the use of a long mask on networks with few hosts and a short mask on subnets with relatively more hosts.

With CIDR, you specify an IP address range using a combination of an IP address and network mask. The CIDR notation has a format like this: xxx.xxx.xxx.xxx/n. Do note that CIDR notation can be used for specifying an address even in non-CIDR networks.

DNS

DNS Domain Name System is for name resolution. You should integrate the DNS Server service with AD DS whenever possible if you have a large network. To do this you should install DNS at the same time that you install AD DS, or install DNS after you install AD DS and then integrate DNS as a separate step. 2008 Server R2 based DNS servers can return both IPv4 host (A) resource records and IPv6 host (AAAA) resource records in response to queries.

DNS performs name-to-IP mapping per the request of the client devices. The DNS namespace must be planned. A common practice is to have one namespace for the internal network and another for external contact. When a new DNS server is not to serve also as a domain controller, you may configure it by first creating a forward and reverse (this is optional) lookup zone, then decide if the server is to allow dynamic updates and whether queries will be forwarded to other servers. You can choose to designate a DNS server on your local network as a forwarder by configuring the forwarding of queries so you may manage name resolution for names that belong to the outside world. A conditional forwarder is one that forwards DNS queries according to the DNS domain name involved. In other words, only some but not all queries will be forwarded.

Windows 2008 R2 based DNS Server service supports incremental zone transfers between servers that need to replicate zone data. This can greatly reduce DNS replication traffic. Directory-integration is preferred since dynamic updates to DNS will be sent to any AD DS-integrated DNS server and will get replicated to all other AD DS-integrated DNS servers via AD DS replication, which is more efficient and reliable. Also, it is possible to use access control list to secure the relevant object container in the directory tree. Because zones will get replicated and synchronized to new domain controllers automatically whenever new installations are introduced, administration will be much easier.

It is very common to install DNS servers on all domain controllers. Generally, it is wise to place these DNS servers at a network location that is centrally accessible to the DNS clients. Performance-wise, the more zones to be handled the more workload to be expected by a DNS server. And don't forget to consider the effects of zone transfer across slower WAN links!

DHCP and LDAP

DHCP Dynamic Host Configuration Protocol is for dynamic IP address configuration. In a modern network you will need them both for ease of administration and scalability. Do note that dynamic addresses allocation is best for frequently changing network topology with a large amount of clients. If you have very few clients, static naming may be acceptable. **Static address assignment is usually preferred for servers.**

A DHCP scope refers to an administrative grouping of IP addresses. An administrator can first create a scope for each physical subnet, then uses the scope to further define the parameters to be used by the clients. A scope has a range of IP addresses, a subnet mask and a scope name. DHCP scope options are configured for assignment to DHCP clients, such as DNS server address, router address, WINS server address, etc. Since each subnet can only have one single DHCP scope with a single continuous range of IP addresses, if you want to use multiple address ranges within a single scope then you will have to carefully configure the required exclusion ranges or conflicts will occur.

LDAP Lightweight Directory Access Protocol refers to the set of protocols for accessing information directories. It is based on the standards contained within the X.500 standard but is deliberately made simpler, so that's why it is sometimes called X.500-lite. It is an open protocol, meaning applications have no need to worry about the type of server hosting the directory.

Wireless Based Local Area Networking

Wireless network relies on RF (Radio Frequency) to function. RF represents any frequency within the electromagnetic spectrum that is associated with radio wave propagation. Most wireless technologies for LAN use are based on RF field propagation. Potential sources of RF interference are microwave ovens, wireless phones, Bluetooth enabled devices and other wireless LANs.

A RF setup involves two parts, which are the transmitter and the receiver. The transmitter takes and encodes the message onto a sine wave for transmission. The receiver receives the radio waves and decodes accordingly. Do remember, Radio transmission ALWAYS requires a clear path between antennas (line of sight LOS).

IEEE 802.11 defines protocol for Ad-hoc and client/server networks. In particular it defines specifications for the physical layer and the Media Access Control layer. A client/server based wireless network uses an access point to control the allocation of transmit time for all wireless stations. The access point is often the target of attackers.

Wired Equivalent Privacy (WEP) is kind of a security protocol for WLAN defined in the 802.11b standard. It is not that secure though as the header and the trailer are not encrypted at all. Typical security attacks against WLANs may include Eavesdropping, RF jamming, and Encryption Cracking. The list keeps growing everyday. Wi-Fi Protected Setup (WPS) is a standard intended for the easy and secure establishment of a wireless home network. To add a new device to the wireless network there can be four choices. They are the PIN Method, the PBC Method, the NFC Method, and the USB Method. Wireless Zero Configuration (WZC) refers to Wireless Auto Configuration (WLAN AutoConfig). It is a wireless connection management utility that comes with Windows XP and later. It works by selecting a wireless network to connect to basing on a user's preferences, even in the absence of a wireless network utility from the NIC manufacturer.

WAN Networking

A WAN covers a relatively broad geographic area that often uses transmission facilities provided by common carriers. It requires quite many different devices to run, EXAMPLES: WAN switches, access servers, modems, CSU/DSUs, and ISDN terminal adapters. A point-to-point link provides a single pre-established WAN communications path from one premise to another. You usually need to have it leased from a carrier or a service provider and thus is often called leased line.

Point-to-Point Protocol PPP is a method for connecting a computer to a remote network, over point-to-point links. It works at the data link layer, and is more stable than SLIP. Most importantly, it has error checking features included.

Many WANs deploy virtual circuits for cost sharing purpose. The two major types of virtual circuits are switched virtual circuits and permanent virtual circuits. Switched circuits allow data connections to be initiated when needed and terminated when completed. Example: ISDN. Packet switching allows users to share common carrier resources continuously without the need for connection initialization all the time. Examples include ATM, Frame Relay and X.25.

Codecs are deployed for compressing data. They are usually lossy, for achieving a relatively small file size. Lossless codecs are available, but the small increase in quality often does not worth the increase in file size. It is in fact possible to have repeated application of lossy codecs for repeated encoding and subsequent decoding, but quality will be degraded quite significantly.

Security planning

The three "As" are often being referred to as the AAA concept. The general types of authentication are:

- Something a person knows (eg. password)

- Something a person has (eg. ID card)

- Something a person is (eg. role and title)

Strong authentication requires two of the above and is known as two-factor authentication. In fact, a major portion of what is required to address nonrepudiation is accomplished through the use of strong methods for authentication and ensuring data integrity. You should also consider to establish written standard business practices for creating a presumption of efficient and reliable operations. Authorization determines if you can carry out the requested actions. Access criteria types include and not limited to:

- Roles

- Groups

- Physical or logical location

- Time of day

- Transaction type

- ... etc

A common practice is to have all access criteria default to "no access" at the very beginning.

Good network security design often follows a top down approach and must reflect the goals, characteristics, and policies of the organizations in which they operate. The primary goals that drive internetworking design and implementation are application availability, cost of ownership and user satisfaction. A top down approach to network design often calls for your understanding of the constraints and objectives of network use as well as the applications and data on which the business relies upon on, before considering the viable internetworking options. It is always recommended that you start your design effort with the business objectives because your network has the most important mission of helping users in achieving business objectives. Once these objectives are well understood, you may proceed further. You shall gain understand on the applications that will be running on the network, the systems that are attached to the network, and the data that will be flow through them.

A proper network security design and implementation plan should outline the required network design tasks on a phase by phase, step by step manner. Within each phase there should be steps that details what are to be done. The advantage of having a proper implementation plan handy is to introduce specific network benefits according to a schedule, thus allowing for proper resource allocation, planning, change control, and configuration and installation. During the design phase, a prototype may be made available for initial testing and review. Before finalizing the new design and putting it into final production use, thorough testing must be done following a well-prepared test plan.

A proper test plan should be in place to address all the key features developed in the planning phase. It should be followed to ensure compatibility with existing system performance as well as to minimize the possibility for delay-causing problems in the deployment stage.

A packet consists of a header which marks the beginning of the packet, a payload of data, and a trailer which marks the end of the packet. The checksum if available for error checking is located at the trailer. The header has to specify the data type in transit. A firewall prevents unauthorized access to or from a private network by examining each message and/or packet that passes through it and blocks those that do not meet the specified security criteria. A packet filter examines each packet entering or leaving the network and accepts or rejects it based on pre-defined security rules. The former uses more sophisticated mechanisms and are more dynamic in nature, but is more expensive and is more costly computing resource-wise. Keep in mind, a firewall doesn't stop viruses. Boot Sector Virus attaches itself to the boot sector of a floppy disk or an executable file and copies all or part of itself onto the boot sector of your hard drive. File-Infecting Virus attaches themselves to executable files associated with other software applications. Macro Virus affects Word and Excel templates. **Windows Server has built-in firewall support.**

Points of Failure and Physical Security

Though the benefits of modern systems, the use of very advanced yet highly sophisticated technologies may present severe continuity issues. Fault-tolerant equipments do have redundant capabilities, but these capabilities won't help if the physical site is compromised (did you watch Die Hard 4.0?).

You need to consider the point(s) of failure you have. A centralized system has everything centrally managed, meaning you have a single point of failure (all risks in one place). With a distributed system you have multiple points of failure (small risks in multiple different places) that are interconnected (the connections themselves could be points of failure too). You need to achieve a proper balance between the two extremes.

Effective physical security measures aim at protecting against unauthorized access, damage, or interference in areas where critical or sensitive information is processed, or where information processing services supporting key business functions are run.

Generally speaking, the following guidelines should always be adhered to:

● The requirements and placement of each physical security barrier should be determined basing on the value of the information or service being protected. They do have to be located away from hazardous processes and/or materials.

- Physical information processing resources must be housed in a secure area capable of protecting the resources from unauthorized physical access, fire, flooding, explosions, and other kinds of disaster.

- Only authorized personnel should be allowed entry into areas that house critical or sensitive information or information processing resources. Facilities where access by unauthorized personnel is to be prevented should require that ID badges be made visible at all times. Personnel should challenge strangers and report their presence to security. Visitors should be escorted only by authorized personnel.

- The award and distribution of passes must be strictly controlled and subject to frequent review. Quarterly reviews have to be performed to ensure that only those individuals with a job related need have access to the computing facilities. Whenever individuals change jobs, their access must be immediately barred.

- Clear Desk Policy should be promoted. Papers and discs should be stored in cabinets when not in use. Sensitive business information should be locked away. Devices for network access should be protected by key locks, passwords and the like (best to have various methods combined). Information processing equipment and media containing highly restricted and confidential data must never be left unattended in public places.

- Off premise devices with classified information must be protected with the proper form of access protection such as passwords, smart cards, and encryption …etc. Damaged storage devices should either be repaired or thoroughly destroyed.

- Adequate power supplies and auxiliary power supplies must be made ready. Uninterruptible Power Source (UPS) should be used to support critical information processing equipments. Power and communications lines should be subject to adequate protection. Cables and cords must be protected from unauthorized interception or damage.

- Air-conditioning units must be sufficient to support the equipments as heat is a huge concern.

- The minimum-security protection activities recommended by the vendor/manufacturer must be implemented.

- Physical emergency procedures must be clearly documented and must be regularly practiced.

- Both manually activated and automatically activated fire suppression equipment must be made ready. If automatic fire suppression system employs water, careful tuning must be performed to avoid damage to critical computer equipments.

- Fire extinguishers should be conveniently placed and well marked. Check them on a periodic basis as they all have expiration dates.

Accounts and Password Management

Passwords serve as the entry point to information system resources. Password management is therefore an important topic. Generally, all accounts that are used to access administrative systems and directory services must have their passwords changed at least once a year. Passwords are not allowed to be changed to the same password currently in use. No password should ever be spoken, written, shared, or in any way made known to anyone (not even the superiors) other than the owner of the account. Passwords must not be shared to allow access to systems while the user is out of office. Alternative temporary accounts should be used when there are resources you need to access while the corresponding user is not in. Also, passwords should never be displayed or concealed within the workspace. User defined passwords must not contain all or part of the user's account name. They must not be the user's name, address, date of birth, username, nickname, or anything that are easy to guess. You may want to use passphrase instead of password. They are typically longer than passwords and can provide effective protection, while still pretty easy to remember.

To ensure successful security awareness training, the factors of Awareness, Training and Education must be considered. Security awareness should be promoted to top management, business managers/users, IT staff and external personnel. It should be done by providing information security education/training, such as via computer-based training or by supplying specialized security awareness material, such as brochures, reference cards, posters and intranet-based electronic documents. Staff should be provided with guidance to help them understand: the meaning of information security, the importance of complying with information security policy and applying associated standards/procedures, and their personal responsibilities for information security.

You need to do your best to maintain security awareness. Use an intranet Web site, posters, newsletters and the like to remind your employees of the importance of information security. You may want to write and post information security FAQs on the Web site and provide an email address for accepting relevant comments and questions. The effectiveness of security awareness should be monitored by measuring the level of security awareness in staff and reviewing it periodically, and the effectiveness of security awareness activities (such as by monitoring the frequency and magnitude of incidents experienced). Security-positive behavior should be encouraged by making attendance at security awareness training compulsory, publicizing security successes and failures throughout the organization, and linking security to personal performance objectives/appraisals.

Disaster Recovery Plans For Servers

Backup copies of the operating system, the application software and all the critical data must be made on a regular basis. The frequency of the backup would depend largely on the frequency of changes made as well as the criticality of the concerned data. A backup copy of the most recent release version of the operating system and the application software should be made available during the process of rebuilding a crashed server. Backup copies of the critical data should be made available when the current data. The data should be backed up on a frequency determined by the user. Generally, application with high transaction volume should have data backups made more frequently.

There are different backup schemes for rotating and replacing backups. A backup rotation scheme refers to a method put in place for effectively backing up data where multiple media are involved in the backup process.

- A First In, First Out FIFO backup scheme involves saving the new or modified files onto the oldest media in a set. It is very simple to use.

- A Grandfather-father-son backup method has been very popular for making tape backups. It involves defining three sets of backups, which are daily (son), weekly (father) and monthly (grand father). The son backups are rotated on a daily basis with one graduating to father status every week. The father backups are rotated on a weekly basis with one graduating to grandfather status every month.

- An incremented media method has a set of numbered media that is being used until the end of the cycle. Then the cycle is repeated using media numbered the same but incremented by one.

- The Towers of Hanoi rotation method is a recursive method which is quite complex to implement.

From a technical perspective, these backup methods are available:

- The Image/block level backup method deals with blocks of data. The backup application will open the disk as a raw disk and then perform logical block-level read and write operations. Backup and restore operations are very fast but no access is allowed during the operation.

- The Application-level backup method is usually application specific. In other words, the backup and restore operations are tightly associated with the application.

- With the Differential Backup method, a differential backup will archive all changes made since the last full backup. The backup process is fast. A full backup, in contrast, is slow to backup but convenient to restore since you only need to have one set of media available.

- File-based incremental backup is typically used when a different set of files is created or modified.

- Direct-attached backup is all about attaching storage devices to the server directly. It remains a very popular topology for backing up servers.

- Network-attached backup works in a LAN. With it, you can have a server on the LAN with a backup device that could be shared by all the servers on the LAN.

- LAN-free backup assumes that a storage area network is in place to provide a high bandwidth between any two devices and offer multiple simultaneous bandwidth capability between multiple pairs of devices.

- With server-free backup, the backup server does not need to spend much effort while the actual backup is accomplished through the data mover agent - the data is moved directly from the source to the backup media without going through the backup server.

Service packs and patches

Your OS and/or your firewall may require patching in order to stay secured. For example, Microsoft release patches to fix vulnerabilities or add security features. Patches should be applied in a consistent and repeatable manner, because failing to patch even a few computers means that the overall network is still vulnerable. Service packs typically include all the essential patching components bundled together for easy downloading. Typically, each new service pack contains all the fixes that are included in previous service packs plus any new fixes, so most of the time you would not need to install a previous service pack before you install the latest one. Do keep in mind, patches may not work perfectly in every environment. Therefore, you should thoroughly test any patches before installing in your environment. To be secure and safe, you might want to have a plan of action to restore the system to its original state if something goes wrong. Backup should be made almost mandatory in such a plan. As of the time of this writing Server 2008 has SP1 released. The link to further information and download is:

http://technet.microsoft.com/en-us/library/ff817647(v=ws.10).aspx

To avoid confusion you want to know that Windows Server 2008 and Windows Server 2008 SP2 are the same operating system at a different service pack level. Windows Server 2008 R2 is in fact the server release of Windows 7, and it is considered "newer" than Windows Server 2008 SP2.

To be precise, Windows Server 2008 is based on the 6.0 kernel, which is the same one used by Windows Vista. Windows Server 2008 R2 is based on the 6.1 kernel, which is the one used by Windows 7.

Server Management UI

Server Manager is the primary console for server configuration and management.

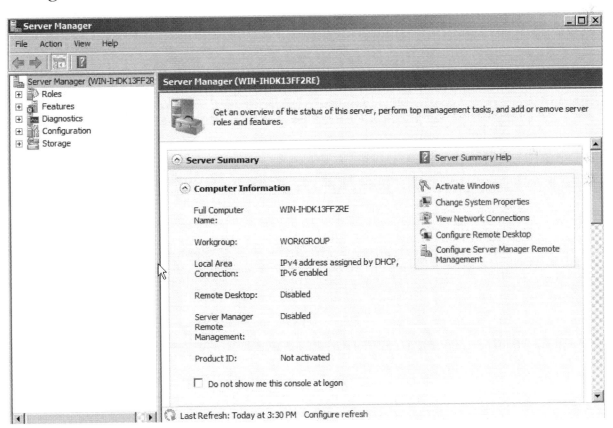

Managing Services

The Services section lists all the available services so you can manage them from a single interface. Right click on anyone of them and there are many settings to play with. For example, you can change the startup type and the account to be used to run the service. Usually a local system account is used for logging on as a service.

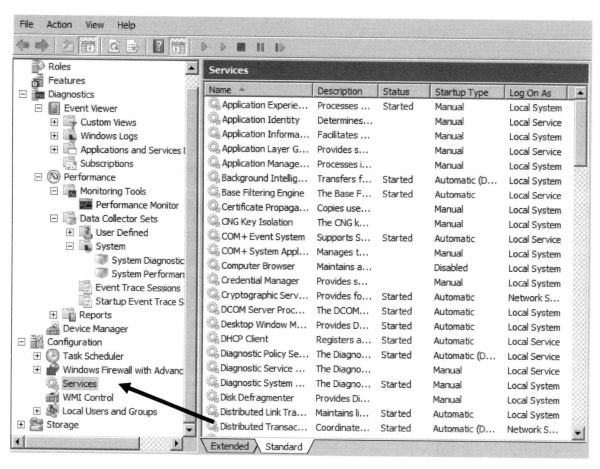

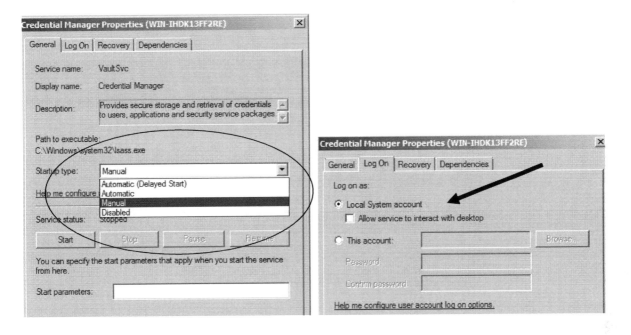

Some of the more critical services are:

- Active Directory Certificate Services allows you to create, distribute, and manage customized public key certificates.

- Active Directory Domain Services are responsible for storing directory data and managing communication between users and domains plus administering user logon processes.

- Active Directory Federation Services provides Web single-sign-on for authenticating web user to multiple Web applications.

- Active Directory Lightweight Directory Services provides support for directory-enabled applications.

- Active Directory Rights Management Services protects information and support AD RMS-enabled applications.

- DNS Services

- DHCP Services

- Remote Desktop Services

- File Services

- Web Server

Other tools and commands that you can use for managing AD are summarized in the coming screen shots – they are pretty much self-explanatory:

Advanced Tools

AD DS Tools

Administer trusts, domain and forest functional levels, and user principal name (UPN) suffixes	AD Domains and Trusts
Query, view, and edit objects and attributes in the directory	ADSI Edit
Add or remove domain controller functionality from a server using the AD DS Installation Wizard	Dcpromo.exe
Perform LDAP operations against the directory such as connect, bind, search, modify, add, and delete	Ldp.exe
Manage computer accounts, domains, and trust relationships	Netdom.exe
Perform database maintenance on the AD DS store, configure AD LDS ports, and view AD LDS instances	Ntdsutil.exe
Troubleshoot and diagnose replication problems between domain controllers	Repadmin.exe

⌄ Directory Services Tools

Add specific types of objects, such as users, groups, and computers, to the directory — Dsadd.exe

Perform maintenance of the AD DS store, configure AD LDS communication ports, and view AD LDS instances — Dsdbutil.exe

View the selected properties of a specific object, such as a user or computer, in the directory — Dsget.exe

Manage application partitions and operations master roles, and remove metadata from abandoned instances — Dsmgmt.exe

Modify an existing object of a specific type, such as a user or computer, in the directory — Dsmod.exe

Move an object to a new location within a domain or rename an existing object in the directory — Dsmove.exe

Query the directory for a specific object type according to specified criteria — Dsquery.exe

Delete an object of a specific type or any general object from the directory — Dsrm.exe

⌄ Networking and Other Tools

Repair domain name dependencies in Group Policy objects and links after a domain rename operation — GPfixup.exe

Configure a client to use a Kerberos V5 realm instead of an AD DS domain — Ksetup.exe

Configure a non-Windows Kerberos service as a security principal in AD DS — Ktpass.exe

Perform troubleshooting tasks such as querying replication status and verifying trust relationships — Nltest.exe

View information on name servers to diagnose DNS infrastructure problems — Nslookup.exe

View settings, manage configuration, and diagnose problems with Windows Time — W32tm.exe

Group Policy and Local Policy

Group Policy can be used to configure computer and user settings on networks based on the Active Directory Domain Services AD DS. For Group Policy to work your network must be based on AD DS, and that the computers you want to manage must be joined to the domain. You must also have the relevant permissions to create and edit the policy objects. Although you can also choose to configure Group Policy settings locally, you should avoid doing that since domain-based Group Policy can centralize management while localized policy cannot.

You may manage all aspects of Group Policy via the Group Policy Management Console GPMC, assuming you have joined a domain. From the interface you can see a list of Group Policy objects GPOs which contain the various policy settings. Do note that GPMC is NOT installed by default so you must add it yourself.

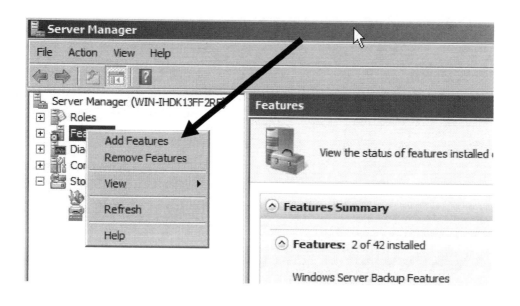

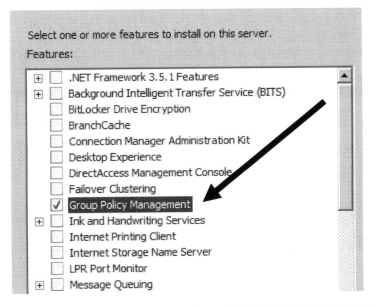

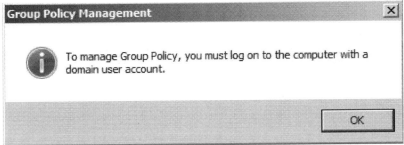

Assuming your computer has been connected to a domain, you may open the GPMC by press the Windows logo key + R to open the RUN dialog box, then enter gpmc.msc and press ENTER. From within the GPMC console tree you can do a lot of things. For example, you can right-click Group Policy Objects in the forest and domain in which you want to create a GPO and then click New to create a new object. You can also add a domain/forest/site here. HOWEVER, adding a domain/site/forest to GPMC does not actually create them in Active Directory. Do remember that GPOs have no impact unless you actually have them linked to a site, a domain, or an OU. At the time you link a GPO to a container, the GPO's settings will be applied to the computers and users in that particular container.

Also don't forget about the concept of inheritance. When you link policies to a container, the child containers will receive them as well.

Within the Computer Configuration and User Configuration folders of the GPMC there are two subfolders, which are Policies and Preferences. The former contains policy settings that Group Policy enforces, while Preferences contains preference settings that can be used to change registry setting, file, folder, and the like... Through preference settings you may configure applications and other Windows features that are not Group Policy compatible.

The local policy editor, on the other hand, may be invoked through gpedit.msc.

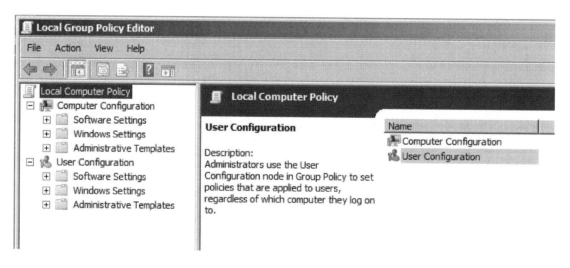

Software Restrictions

Software restriction policies can be found within the Local Security Policy Editor. Check out the left pane and you will see it there.

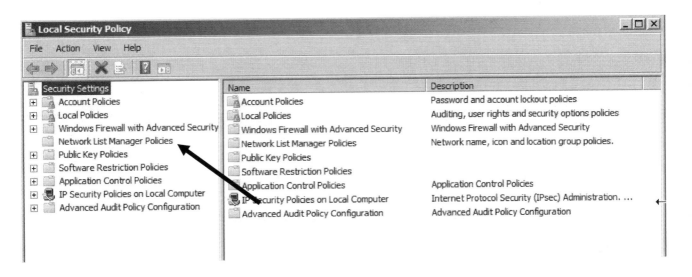

A rule can be Unrestricted or Disallowed. You may have a software restriction policy applied to allow only this list of trusted applications, OR specifically disallow those undesired applications or file types that should be prohibited. By default there is no rule or policy in there.

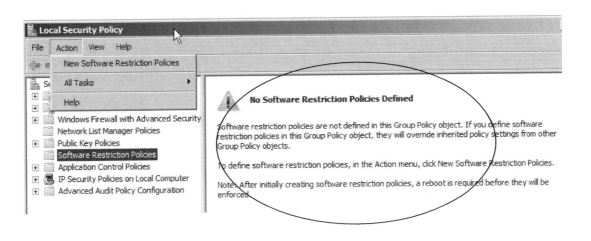

Basic User is kind of a in-between default rule that allows users to execute applications that don't really require administrative privileges. With this rule in place, if you want to allow users to run applications with administrative privileges then you must have a specific rule created.

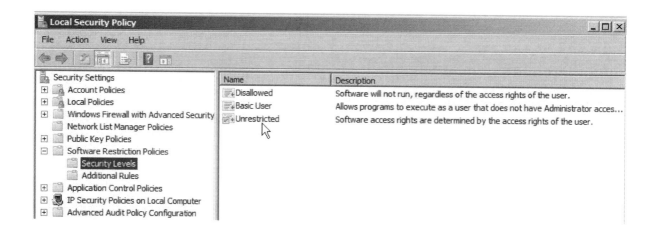

Software Restriction Policies rely on four different types of rule to identify software, which are Hash, Certificate, Path and Zone (Internet zone, as specified in Internet Explorer - in fact this rule applies primarily to Windows Installer packages which may be downloaded through the Internet explorer.). Do realize that these policies will not prevent restricted processes that run under the name of the System account. Different rules do have different drawbacks. Hash rule are specific to files so if you need to hash many files you will have to work on each file one by one. Path Rules cannot be used on folders and files that can change location. Certificate rules are vendor specific so flexibility is lacking when you have different programs from the same vendor. You do want to know that it is possible for rules to have conflicts. The most specific rules take precedence. Remember this order:

1. Hash rules are the most specific!

2. Certificate rules

3. Path rules

4. Zone rules

5. Default rules are the least specific!

The Enforcement Properties policy can be used to specify whether to apply default rules to all files, including libraries or all files excluding libraries. Libraries mean DLLs. Some DLLs can be dangerous!

AppLocker

Applocker (from within the Local Security Policy Editor) can be used to configure Application Control Policies so you may choose to block the execution of a software as you see fit. You can have AppLocker rules associated with a specific user or group within an organization. No rules are in place by default. Default rules, if any, should NOT be used for production purpose. You should use the default rules as a template when creating your very own rules only. You also want to know that unlike Software Restriction Policies, an AppLocker rule collection would only function as an allowed list of files, which means only those files that are listed would be allowed to run.

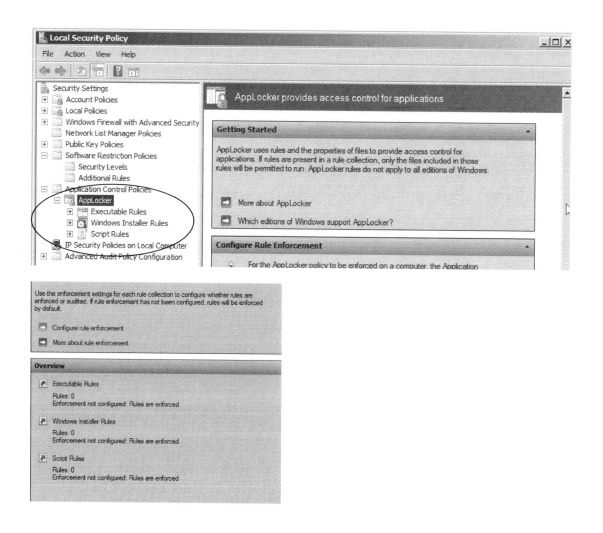

DLL rule collection covers .dll and also .ocx files. The possible defaults are Allows members of the local Administrators group to run all DLLs; Allow all users to run DLLs in the Windows folder; and Allow all users to run DLLs in the Program Files folder. DLL rules may affect system performance! Executable rules cover files with only .exe and .com. Windows Installer rules cover .msi and .msp files. Script rules cover all these:

- .ps1

- .bat

- .cmd

- .vbs

- .js

AppLocker has a feature to export and import AppLocker policies as an XML file so you may test and modify the policy outside your production environment. After exporting the policy to an XML file, you can import it onto a reference computer for further editing.

Running a program as an administrator

User Account Control UAC is a feature that can limit privileges of users by default. For the command line to be run as an administrator, right click the icon for the command prompt and choose Run as administrator.

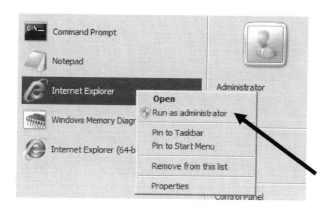

The Run this program as an administrator option may not always be available. When you don't see this option, it could be that:

- the application is blocked from running elevated

- the application does not require administrative credentials to run

- you are not logged on as administrator

Administrator Account

When you set up Windows Server, you need to use a local administrator account that allows you to set up the computer and install the necessary programs. **You have no way to delete this account.** BEWARE: A local administrator is an admin with full rights over the local machine only. A Domain Administrator has admin rights access over the entire domain. The Enterprise Admin is said to have God rights everywhere in the network. Keep in mind, after installation you must set a complex password for this account. The password must be a complex one, with letters, numbers and symbols included. You may also use this command to require password and take the chance to change to a strong password: net user Administrator <password>/passwordreq:yes . MS defines a "strong password" as one which is at least seven characters long and without using user name, real name, company name or complete dictionary word. It should also be one significantly different from previous passwords (if any). You may in fact create passwords that contain characters from the extended ASCII character set, which can increase the number of characters that you may use when creating a password.

You also have the option to create a password reset disk. Note that a password reset disk can only be used for local computer accounts. You cannot use it for domain accounts. You also cannot change your password and create a password reset disk at the same time. HOWEVER, you are free to change your password any time after creating a password reset disk. Other changes related to the administrator account and other user accounts can be made via the Server Manager:

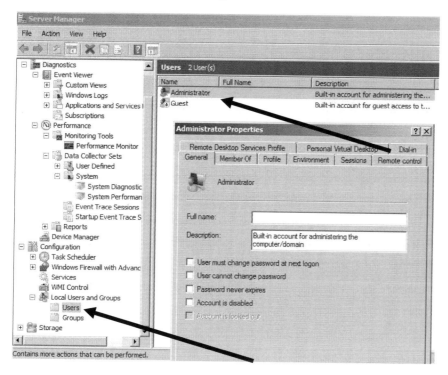

Questions:

1. You may manage all aspects of Group Policy via which interface?

2. Software restriction policies can be found within which interface?

3. What are the primary functions of the Active Directory Certificate Services?

4. What are the primary functions of the Active Directory Domain Services?

5. What are the primary functions of the Active Directory Federation Services?

6. What are the primary functions of the Active Directory Lightweight Directory Services?

7. Software Restriction Policies rely on four different types of rule to identify software, which are:

8. Applocker can be used to configure:

9. DLL rule collection covers what files?

10. What is UAC for?

11. What is the limitation of the password reset disk?

12. The _____ Admin is said to have God rights everywhere in the network.

Answers:

1. *You may manage all aspects of Group Policy via the Group Policy Management Console GPMC, assuming you have joined a domain.*

2. *Software restriction policies can be found within the Local Security Policy Editor.*

3. *Active Directory Certificate Services allows you to create, distribute, and manage customized public key certificates.*

4. *Active Directory Domain Services are responsible for storing directory data and managing communication between users and domains plus administering user logon processes.*

5. *Active Directory Federation Services provides Web single-sign-on for authenticating web user to multiple Web applications.*

6. *Active Directory Lightweight Directory Services provides support for directory-enabled applications.*

7. *Software Restriction Policies rely on four different types of rule to identify software, which are Hash, Certificate, Path and Zone.*

8. *Applocker can be used to configure Application Control Policies so you may choose to block the execution of a software as you see fit.*

9. *DLL rule collection covers .dll and also .ocx files.*

10. *User Account Control UAC is a feature that can limit privileges of users by default.*

11. *A password reset disk can only be used for local computer accounts. You cannot use it for domain accounts.*

12. *The Enterprise Admin is said to have God rights everywhere in the network.*

Network Settings, Security and Remote/Mobile Access

Network Location

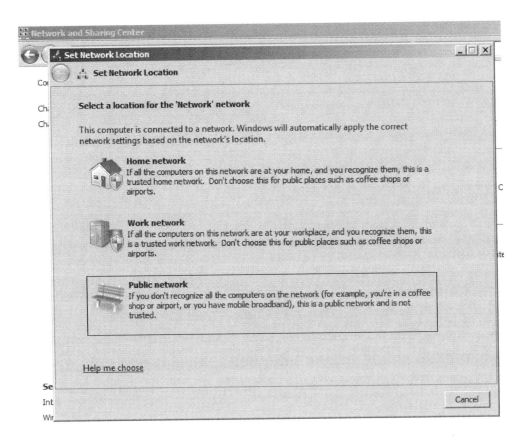

Network location is a profile containing a collection of network and sharing settings which can be applied to the network you are connected to. Windows Server has 3 different types of network categories, which are Public, Private and Domain-authenticated. The Set Network Location dialog provides 3 network locations, which are Public, Work and Home. Domain networks by default are automatically set to the Domain Authenticated category. In fact, connecting a computer to a domain network will automatically set the network category to domain authenticated.

Private category, on the other hand, is divided into Work and Home locations, which are primarily for internal Windows configuration. Note that on a domain-joined computer changing the network location will not require administrative privileges. However, on a non-domain-joined computer changing the network location will require administrative privileges.

Network Location and Windows Firewall are in theory mutually independent. In practice, however, the configuration of Windows Firewall would largely be based on the current network category or categories. When connected to a Public network, only Core Networking rules will be enabled. However, when connected to a Private network, rules of Core Networking, Network Discovery, and Remote Assistance are all enabled.

IP v4 and v6

Windows Server 2008 R2 supports both IPv4 and IPv6. Both of them are installed and enabled by default. It is possible to tunnel IPv6 traffic through an IPv4 network. It is also possible to tunnel IPv4 traffic across an IPv6 network.

There are transition technologies you may consider if you are not ready for IPv6 entirely. ISATAP allows unicast communication between IPv6/IPv4 hosts across your IPv4 intranet. 6to4 allows unicast communication to take place between IPv6/IPv4 hosts and IPv6-capable sites through the Internet. Teredo is similar to 6to4 and can work even when there are private IPv4 addresses and NAT devices involved. IP-HTTPS permits IPv6 to be tunneled using HTTP with SSL as a transport.

Network Sharing and Discovery

The Network and Sharing Center is an interface for basic networking setup. Network discovery, connection status and file sharing are all available here.

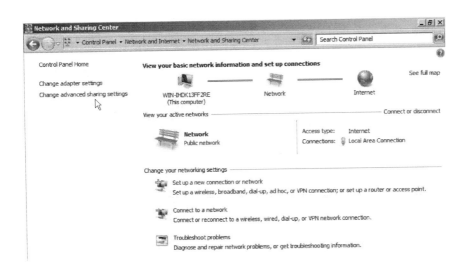

Status of the network adaptors can be viewed by right clicking on the desired adaptor and choose status. Initial troubleshooting can be performed via the Diagnose option.

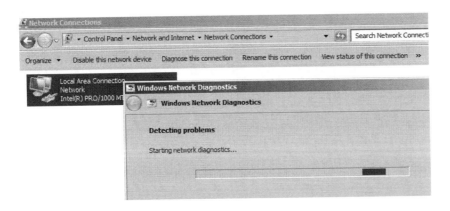

Before you may share files and folders, first you must log in as an Administrator and must make sure that all the relevant systems are connected on the same workgroup. To view the workgroup of the client computer, open the Computer Properties dialog from its Control Panel.

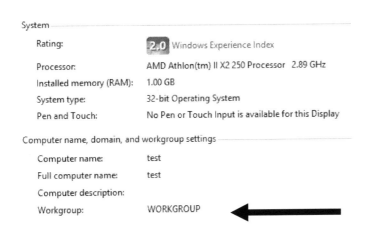

In fact you can always change the computer name and the workgroup name from there:

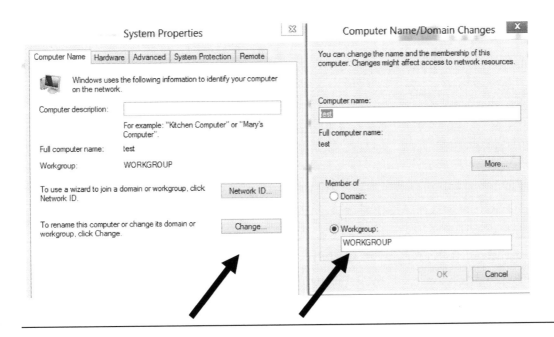

Network Discovery allows the computer to automatically search for other devices on the network. It also works the other around - other computers on the same network can find your computer. An On state allows your computer to see other network computers and devices and also allows people on other network computers to see you. An Off state prevents your computer from seeing others and also prevents people on other network computers from seeing you. A custom state is a mixed state. When you have Network Discovery enabled, the Windows OS becomes immediately discoverable on the network although it would not allow other computers to communicate or access information stored in it. To make the computer accessible from the network, you need to manually enable File and Printer Sharing.

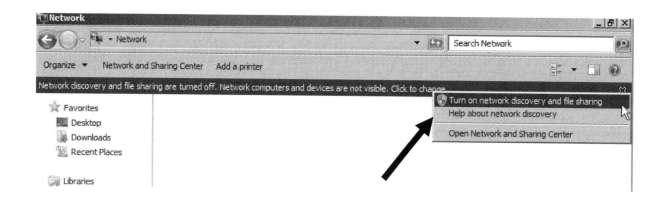

File and Print Services

The File Server Resource Manager MMC snap-in can be used to manage storage resources on local or remote servers. You may set soft or hard space limits on a volume or folder tree. OR you may create and apply quota templates with standard quota properties. You may create filter rules to block attempts by users to save certain file types on a volume or folder tree. You may even create and apply screening templates as needed. There are also built-in reports for tracking quota usage, file screening activity, and patterns of storage use.

The File Services role also comes with the Storage Manager for SANs, which can be used to create and manage logical unit numbers on Fibre Channel and Internet SCSI disk drive subsystems that support Virtual Disk Service V1.1 or later. Support for Distributed File System DFS is also available. DFS Namespaces allows you to group shared folders that are located on different servers into one or more logically structured namespaces, while DFS Replication allows you to keep folders synchronized between servers across very sow and weak network connections.

With the Print Services role in place, it is possible to use Print Management with Group Policy to automatically deploy printer connections. Per-user printer connections during background Group Policy refresh operations is fully supported assuming you have Vista or later as the client side OS. You may use the Printer Migration Wizard or the Printbrm.exe utility to export print queues, printer settings, printer ports, and language monitors, and later import them onto another older print server for backward compatibility support.

You can use the Share and Storage Management console to manage shared sessions and files in real time – you can see who is using your share/file in real time and terminate any session as needed.

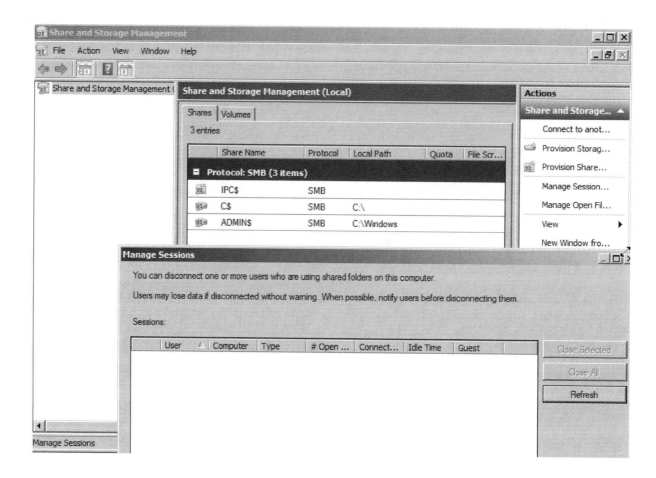

Name Resolution

Windows Server name resolution can take place via these methods:

- local hosts file located in C:\Windows\System32\drivers\etc\

- DNS lookup

- Link-Local Multicast Name Resolution LLMNR

- NetBIOS name query request within a small network

The hosts file holds a list of ip addresses and the corresponding host name. The file needs to be updated by hand on a per machine basis, which is not preferable. LLMNR is a Microsoft protocol for those private networks that have no DNS server. It can allow private networks to operate as IP networks without requiring the various hosts within it to be configured with addresses. It works by sending multicasts UDP messages via port 5355. Since it requires hosts to transmit multicast LLMNR packets which identify the hosts, security may be at risk. You may use Group policy to disable LLMNR. You may also edit the registry to achieve the same. NetBIOS should only be treated as a measure for very small network or for backward compatibility.

Command line networking tools

Command line tools such as ipconfig, ping, tracert …etc remain the same across Windows versions. When used with the /all option the ipconfig tool can show a detailed configuration report for all interfaces, wired and wireless. /flushdns is an option that can delete the DNS name cache. /registerdns is an option that can refresh all DHCP leases and even re-register the DNS names. /displaydns is an option that can show the contents of the DNS resolver cache. /release and /renew are options that you can use to release and renew the DHCP-allocated IP address. /renew6 is for renewing IPv6 DHCP lease. You do need to specify the adaptor you are referring to when renewing address leases. Nslookup is for troubleshooting DNS problems, particularly host name resolution. You may in fact set the local computer into the debug mode by using set debug or set d2. The latter gives even more details. Tracert is a route tracing tool capable of showing a list of near-side only router interfaces along the path between a source and a destination. It uses the IP TTL field in the ICMP Echo Requests and ICMP Time Exceeded messages to determine the correct path. For it to work as expected you may need to turn off ICMP filtering. The ping command can send an ICMP Echo Request to a destination IP address. It is the most basic tool for determining connectivity.

```
C:\Users\mike>ping 127.0.0.1

Pinging 127.0.0.1 with 32 bytes of data:
Reply from 127.0.0.1: bytes=32 time<1ms TTL=128
Reply from 127.0.0.1: bytes=32 time<1ms TTL=128
Reply from 127.0.0.1: bytes=32 time<1ms TTL=128
Reply from 127.0.0.1: bytes=32 time<1ms TTL=128

Ping statistics for 127.0.0.1:
    Packets: Sent = 4, Received = 4, Lost = 0 (0% loss),
Approximate round trip times in milli-seconds:
    Minimum = 0ms, Maximum = 0ms, Average = 0ms

C:\Users\mike>
```

The PathPing tool is a route tracing tool with features from both Ping and Tracert. It has a default number of hops set to 30 plus a default wait time before a time-out set to 3000 milliseconds. Netdiag is an advanced tool you can use to isolate networking and connectivity problems. It offers MANY tests to determine the state of a network client, including:

Network Adapter Status	NetWare test	Kerberos Test
IP Configuration	IPX test	LDAP Test
Domain Membership	IPSec test	Route test
Transports Test	WINS Service Test	NetStat test
APIPA Address	Winsock Test	Bindings test
IP Loopback Ping	DNS Test	WAN test
Default Gateway	Redirector and Browser Test	Modem test

NetBT Name Test	DC Discovery Test	NetWare test
	DC List Test	IPX test
	Trust Relationship Test	IPSec test

Windows Firewall and IP Security Policy

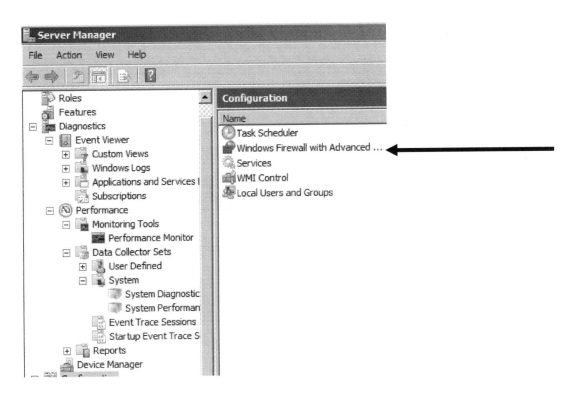

As a stateful host-based firewall, Windows Firewall can be configured via the Windows Firewall with Advanced Security MMC snap-in or the Netsh advfirewall command. You may also access it via the Control Panel. However, configuration via the Control Panel is mostly for typical end user tasks. Advanced tasks should be performed via the MMC snap-in.

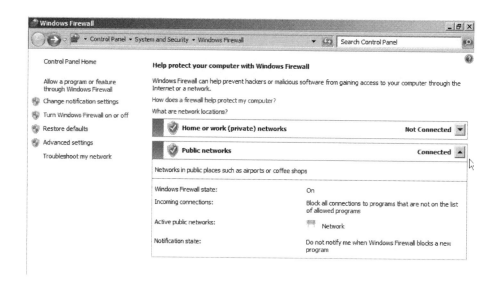

You should determine what windows services and third party programs should be allowed to communicate between different network locations.

Allow programs to communicate through Windows Firewall

To add, change, or remove allowed programs and ports, click Change settings.

What are the risks of allowing a program to communicate?

Change settings

Allowed programs and features:

Name	Home/Work (Private)	Public
BranchCache - Content Retrieval (Uses HTTP)	☐	☐
BranchCache - Hosted Cache Client (Uses HTTPS)	☐	☐
BranchCache - Hosted Cache Server (Uses HTTPS)	☐	☐
BranchCache - Peer Discovery (Uses WSD)	☐	☐
COM+ Network Access	☐	☐
COM+ Remote Administration	☐	☐
☑ Core Networking	☑	☑
☑ DFS Management	☑	☑
Distributed Transaction Coordinator	☐	☐
File and Printer Sharing	☐	☐
iSCSI Service	☐	☐
Key Management Service	☐	☐
Netlogon Service	☐	☐
Network Discovery	☐	☐

Details...   Remove

Allow another program...

At the netsh advfirewall context, the firewall sub command allows you to change to the Netsh AdvFirewall Firewall context so you can view, create, and modify firewall rules. The possible commands are add, delete, set and show. Direction of traffic is either in or out, while action can be allow, block or bypass. On the other hand, if you invoke the command mainmode at the netsh advfirewall context, you can change to the netsh advfirewall mainmode context for viewing, creating, and modifying main mode rules that deal with how IPsec negotiates security associations between computers.

You use firewall rules to allow the server computer to send traffic to, or receive traffic from, programs, system services, computers, or users. Firewall rules can be created to allow the connection, allow a connection only if it is secured through IPsec, or block the connection entirely.

Rules may be for either inbound traffic or outbound traffic and may specify the computers or users, program, service, port, protocol and the type of network adapter involved. In fact it is possible for you to configure a firewall rule to be applied only if the IPv4/IPv6 addresses involved match certain specified local and remote addresses.

The default rule processing behavior is to block all unsolicited inbound network traffic and at the same time allowing all outbound network traffic. You may change the default behavior for the Domain Profile, Private Profile, and Public Profile. Do note that you may use program rules to allow unsolicited incoming traffic through the Windows Firewall only if the program uses Winsock for making port assignments.

There are three profiles for Windows Firewall with Advanced Security, which are Domain (to be applied to a network adapter when it is connected to a network on which it can find a domain controller), Private (to be applied to a network adapter when it is connected to a network identified as a private network behind a security device), and Public. When the profile is not Domain or Private, the default would be Public. With Windows Server 2008 R2, multiple active per-network adapter profiles can be supported.

Firewall rules are either locally stored or save in GPOs. The Windows Service Hardening rule can restrict services from establishing connections in ways not intended out of the box. Connection security rules define authentication using IPsec and enforce Network Access Protection NAP policy.

Authenticated bypass rules allow connections and bypass other inbound rules when the traffic is protected with IPsec. Block rules aim to explicitly blocks a particular type of traffic, and can be used to override a matching allow rule. Allow rules can explicitly allow a particular type of traffic. Default rules define the kind of action to take when a connection does not meet any of the higher order rules. Within each rule category, rules are matched by the specificity - the more specific rules get applied.

IP Security Policies can be created via the Local Policy Editor. There is an IP Security Policy snap-in for backward compatibility. You may use it to create IPsec policies that can be applied to computers running Vista, Windows Server 2008, Windows 7, and Windows Server 2008 R2, although the newest security algorithms and features are not supported.

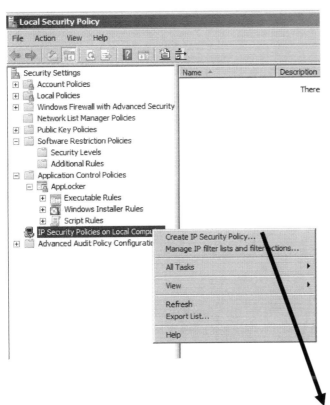

Welcome to the IP Security Policy Wizard

This wizard helps you create an IP Security policy. You will specify the level of security to use when communicating with specific computers or groups of computers (subnets), and for particular IP traffic types.

To continue, click Next.

IPSec and SSL

To prevent messages from being intercepted during transmission over the network, technologies like IPSec and SSL should be considered. They make it very time consuming to hack. Frankly, attackers love to attack a weak spot in a system than to touch a heavily fortified component. They are not likely to attack encrypted information communicated in a network because it would be VERY time consuming. Instead, the endpoints (e.g. the servers and the clients) are often the much easier targets.

IPsec is different from SSL in that it runs at layer 3, so it can protect both TCP and UDP traffic. SSL operates from the transport layer up so less flexibility can be offered. The goal of SSL is to provide endpoint authentication as well as communications privacy via cryptography.

Disk based encryption

Whole Disk Encryption protects all data on an entire computer disk drive. The engine behinds it operates at the system level that is between the operating system and the disk drive, thus providing totally transparent sector-by-sector disk encryption in background. There are commercial software for this purpose. Windows also offer the EFS Encryption File System for similar use. EFS does support encryption on a per folder basis.

When you choose to encrypt the parent folder, all files and subfolders that are to be added in the future will be encrypted. When you choose to encrypt all files and subfolders when you encrypt a folder, all files and subfolders currently in the folder as well as any files and subfolders that are to be added in the future will be encrypted. When you choose to encrypt the folder only, files and subfolders currently in the folder will not be encrypted.

Encrypting File System certificates allow the certificate holder to use EFS to encrypt and decrypt data. Ordinary EFS users should be granted this type of certificate. File Recovery certificates are for recovering encrypted files and folders. Domain admins and/or designated data recovery agents should be granted this type of certificate. You should use the Certificates MMC snap-in to back up the default recovery keys. Do so before you make any changes to the default recovery policy!

Firewall security

Firewall configuration, administration and operational procedures should always be well documented. Configuration of multiple firewalls used in parallel (if any) must be identical. Integrity checking of the configuration files of the firewall using checksums should be performed whenever applicable. Log recording and review for the firewall should be done regularly. Backups of the system and configuration files for firewall must be regularly taken. And keep in mind, proper maintenance of user accounts is highly important.

You must be aware that firewall is never the totality of a security solution. There are a number of threats that a firewall cannot protect against, including:

- Denial of service attacks and assure data integrity
- Attacks from unwitting users
- Attacks from computer virus or malicious code

On the other hand you want to know that the boundary between firewall and other security measures is becoming increasingly blurred as firewall manufacturers continuously incorporate additional features. A lot of the modern routers, for example, are having basic firewall functions and features. Always remember, routers should be properly configured to deny all traffic by default, and to allow only permitted traffic to go through. Source routing should be disabled. Logging, backup and other administrative tasks should be properly performed similar to those for the firewall.

Virus security

Virus always poses a problem, and you may need a separate host machine to be set up to connect with the firewall to check for computer viruses and malicious codes in all incoming traffic when going through the firewall. This can centralize the control in updating individual computer virus and/or malicious code patterns, and prevent the computer virus or malicious codes from entering into the web or mail servers. Anti-virus software and malicious code detection and repair software may as well be incorporated with the mail server or the web server to specifically protect individual servers.

Windows Firewall does not stop viruses!

Web server security

If you are running Web Servers, separate web servers should be used to restrict access when providing different information to internal and external users. Web servers may be placed inside or outside the internal network. Web servers, which are placed inside the internal network, are normally used for providing information to internal users, while outside servers are used for disseminating information to the public or external users. All outside web servers need to be connected to the firewall in the DMZ with a separate network interface. Ideally a dedicated host should be assigned for running a web server, a mail server or any critical service. The reason is simple - in case of being compromised, this can reduce the impact to other services.

IIS is always vulnerable to attacks!

Name resolution security

All host names and addresses stored in an external DNS are supposed to be exposed to public. Hence, the external DNS should not hold information about the internal network. The external DNS may also be hosted at the ISP. A separate internal DNS server should be set up and placed in the internal network if internal domain information need not be disclosed to the Internet.

Remote Management

Remote Desktop RDP is a feature that allows one to connect to the work computer from a remote location, exactly like using VNC. On the client side, to enable the remote desktop connection feature on a typical client such as Windows 7 so the computer can accept incoming request, click Start -> right click the Computer option -> Properties -> Remote settings -> System

Properties -> Allow connections from computers running any version of Remote Desktop. To initiate a connection, choose Start -> All Programs -> Accessories -> Remote Desktop Connection. You need to provide the destination IP address, user name and password.

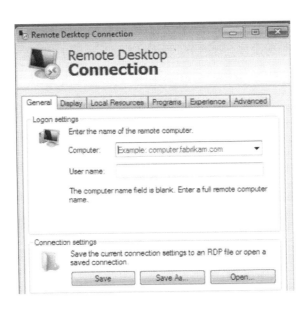

Do note that Remote Desktop is usually not enabled by default on the client. Also, if your remote connection is behind a router or a firewall, make sure connections on port 3389 are allowed. If you want to perform remote server management from Windows 7, you should consider to use the Remote Server Administration Tools RSAT. Through the RSAT tools you can manage computers running Server 2008 R2, Server 2008, or Server 2003. By default the tools would only open those ports and enables only those services that are required for remote management to function.

SERVER SIDE - To install and configure a Remote Desktop Session Host RD Session Host server, you need to add the RD Session Host role service to your Windows Server 2008 R2 computer. You can use Server Manager to achieve this. For your users to connect to this server, don't forget to add the user accounts to the local Remote Desktop Users group. In fact, you can configure a remote desktop services profile for each individual user account:

The Remote Desktop Gateway RD Gateway role service can allow authorized remote users to connect to those RDP accessible resources hosted on the internal corporate networks from Remote Desktop Connection RDC client. When planning to use this role keep in mind that response time would be the key metric for performance measurement. It tells the time taken for a data packet to travel from the RDC through the

Gateway server to the RD Session Host server and then return back to the RDC.

Folder Redirection and Offline Access

Folder redirection allows users and administrators to redirect the path of a folder to a new location. Redirection can be done either manually or through using Group Policy. The new location can be a local folder or a directory somewhere on the network.

On the CLIENT SIDE - In Windows 7, synchronization of offline files take place automatically in the background so there is no need to manually choose between online and offline modes. Windows 7 is capable of redirecting user folders to the proper network location and automatically synchronizes the files. When the user logs off the network, Windows 7 will open the local copies instead. You need to share the folder on the server before you can enable caching for offline file operation. You also need to enable caching on the client computer by mapping a network drive or browsing the network for locating the shared folder. You can right click on the folder and choose "Always Available Offline."

On the SERVER SIDE - You can configure Offline Files through the Offline Files policies GPO. Four of the policies are particularly useful (based on their names you should know their meanings):

● Subfolders always available offline

- Limit disk space used by offline files

- Allow or Disallow use of the Offline Files feature

- Encrypt the Offline Files cache

If sync conflicts occur due to the fact that changes are made to files available offline both on the file server and on the local cache, you will need to use the Sync Center to get them resolved. You can choose to keep the local version, keep the server version or keep both versions, with the local copy being renamed.

Offline Files can make network files available even when a network connection to the server is either unavailable or is very slow. In any case, based on MS' recommendation, you should create a root share on the server and then let the system create the users' folders, then synchronize files at logoff when using Folder Redirection with Offline Files. Since the redirected folders may contain personal information, you want to create a security group for those users who have redirected folders on a particular share and accordingly limit access only to those users. You want to create a hidden share by using a dollar sign ($) after the share name. And you should only grant users the minimum permissions necessary for accessing the data. Do not rely only on EFS. EFS can encrypt files on a remote server only while it is stored on the disk, but not when it is transmitted across the network. You do want to encrypt the offline file cache. You can do so via Group Policy - check out the Computer Configuration\Administrative Templates\Network\Offline Files node in the Group Policy Object Editor snap-in. OR, click Folder Options on the Tools menu from within Windows Explorer. Click on Offline Files, and then check the Encrypt offline files to secure data check box.

DirectAccess, Remote Access and Routing

DirectAccess aims to allow connectivity to the corporate network without the need for using traditional VPN connections. It supports domain-joined Windows 7 Enterprise and Ultimate edition clients as well as Windows 8 clients. Earlier clients are not supported.

A complete DirectAccess solution for mobile access requires a DirectAccess server running Windows Server 2008 R2 with dual network adapters - one facing the internet another facing the intranet. The former needs to have two consecutive public IPv4 addresses assigned. There must also be a domain controller and DNS server running Windows Server 2008 SP2 or Windows Server 2008 R2, plus a public key infrastructure issuing computer certificates. The client computers must be running Windows 7 Enterprise or Windows 7 Ultimate and must be members of the AD DS domain. Think of it as a better and user friendlier way of using VPN for remote connections.

DirectAccess makes use of IPsec for authentication (in fact, authentication takes place before the user logs on) and encryption of communications across the Internet. A major requirement for DirectAccess to work is that IPv6 must be implemented. If IPv6 is not yet deployed, you will need to use transition technologies. You may also use a NAT64 device to translate IPv6 and IPv4 traffics. When there is a firewall or proxy server that prevents the client from using 6to4 or Teredo to reach the DirectAccess server, the client will automatically connect via IP-HTTPS. You may use Nltest.exe at the command line with the options /dsgetdc: /force for DirectAccess troubleshooting. You may determine whether DirectAccess clients,

DirectAccess servers, and other intranet resources can actually contact your domain controllers for IPsec authentication. Do note that the DirectAccess Management Console is a feature that has to be manually installed. It is not installed by default.

Select one or more features to install on this server.
Features:
- ☐ .NET Framework 3.5.1 Features
- ☐ Background Intelligent Transfer Service (BITS)
- ☐ BitLocker Drive Encryption
- ☐ BranchCache
- ☐ Connection Manager Administration Kit
- ☐ Desktop Experience
- ☐ DirectAccess Management Console

The Microsoft DirectAccess Connectivity Assistant DCA as part of the Windows Optimized Desktop Toolkit 2010 is a tool that can inform mobile users of their connectivity status and provide tools to help them reconnect if necessary. It can also create diagnostics to ease the troubleshooting problem.

The Routing and Remote Access service RRAS has two major functions. It allows you to deploy VPN connections to provide end users with remote access to the corporate network. It also allows you to create a site-to-site VPN connection between two servers. On the other hand, it allows your server to act as a software router and/or a network address translator.

In Windows Server 2008 R2, a server computer may be configured to run with the RRAS server role. Packet filtering on a given interface is possible, and can be enabled via Windows firewall or inbound/outbound filters of

RRAS. Don't use both together. The RRAS Packet Filter is a stateless mechanism. It is configurable through the RRAS MMC snap-in , the netsh based scripting mechanism or the remote access policies.

To install RRAS, through Server Manager you go to Roles Summary and click Add roles. When selecting Server Roles, choose Network Policy and Access Services. Then pick Routing and Remote Access Services. After installing the RRAS server role, it is initially in a disabled state so you must enable it manually.

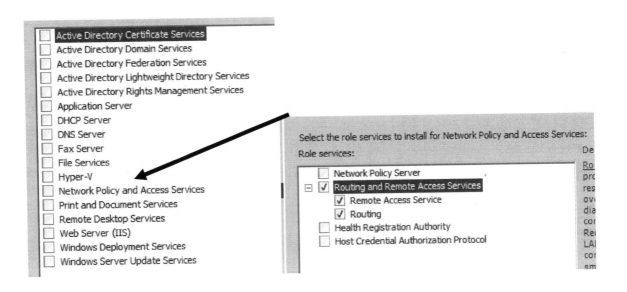

From within the RRAS MMC Snap-in you should right click on the server name and click Configure and Enable Routing and Remote Access. This will call up the configuration wizard for it.

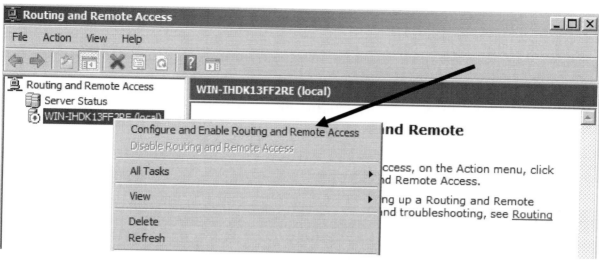

Routing and Remote Access

File   Action   View   Help

Routing and Remote Access
Server Status
WIN-IHDK13FF2RE (local)

Configure and Enable Routing and Remote Access
Disable Routing and Remote Access

All Tasks   ▶

View   ▶

Delete
Refresh

WIN-IHDK13FF2RE (local)

nd Remote

ccess, on the Action menu, click
nd Remote Access.

ng up a Routing and Remote
nd troubleshooting, see Routing

Routing and Remote Access Server Setup Wizard

**Welcome to the Routing and Remote
Access Server Setup Wizard**

This wizard helps you set up your server so that you can
connect to other networks and allow connections from
remote clients.

To continue, click Next.

Routing and Remote Access Server Setup Wizard

Configuration

You can enable any of the following combinations of services, or you can
customize this server.

○ Remote access (dial-up or VPN)

Allow remote clients to connect to this server through either a dial-up connection or a
secure virtual private network (VPN) Internet connection.

○ Network address translation (NAT)

Allow internal clients to connect to the Internet using one public IP address.

○ Virtual private network (VPN) access and NAT

Allow remote clients to connect to this server through the Internet and local clients to
connect to the Internet using a single public IP address.

○ Secure connection between two private networks

Connect this network to a remote network, such as a branch office.

○ Custom configuration

Select any combination of the features available in Routing and Remote Access.

For more information

Remote Access may be as dial-up or through VPN. If it serves as a VPN server, remember that it needs a machine certificate to create SSL VPN connection with the SSL VPN client, and that the common name on the certificate must match the name that the VPN client uses for making the connection.

You should NOT use DHCP to configure a VPN server. It is recommended that you manually configure TCP/IP or use DHCP with MAC address reservations so that the TCP/IP configuration of the VPN server can be kept stable.

In terms of user authentication, through the Managing Multiple Remote Access Servers page you may select whether you want to use a centralized RADIUS server. If you choose No, then RRAS will use its local account database or the domain account database if it is a member of AD. In terms of logging, these are the available options:

- Log errors only.

- Log errors and warnings.

- Log all events.

- Do not log any events.

- Log additional Routing and Remote Access information (used for debugging). This option can drag down performance quite significantly.

To allow RRAS to function as a router, you should enable and configure RIP via the RRAS MMC snap-in. For IPv4, RIP Version 2 for Internet Protocol is the choice. You should add it, then right-click RIP and choose New Interface. You should select the interface that is connected to a subnet on which the remote router is connected so your interface can communicate with it through RIP. For security purpose you want to be careful about accpeting routing updates from other routers. Possible options are:

- Accept announcements from all routers - this is the default.

- Accept announcements from listed routers only - recommended.

- Ignore announcements from all listed routers

RRAS supports NAT. HOWEVER, since NAT already includes addressing and name resolution features that provide DHCP and DNS services to clients, you should not run DHCP service or DHCP Relay Agent with NAT addressing enabled. You should also NOT run the DNS service if NAT TCP/IP networking name resolution is currently enabled.

BranchCache

BranchCache is officially a WAN bandwidth optimization technology. In fact it is nothing other than a smart file caching service. With it, after a client has downloaded a piece of content, other clients that look for the same content can retrieve content information identifiers and accordingly find the content in the local office where the content is cached. Hosted cache mode is for branch office with a cache server while distributed cache mode is for a server-less environment. Types of content server include File server, Web server and Application server.

Do note that BranchCache can be deployed in a domain-based or non-domain based environment, as long as a VPN or DirectAccess connection is available between the content servers and the branch office. Also note that it is NOT a feature installed by default so you must add it yourself.

```
Select one or more features to install on this server.
Features:

  ⊞ ☐  .NET Framework 3.5.1 Features                      ▲
  ⊞ ☐  Background Intelligent Transfer Service (BITS)
    ☐  BitLocker Drive Encryption
    ☐  BranchCache          ◄──────────────
    ☐  Connection Manager Administration Kit
    ☐  Desktop Experience
```

Bitlocker

BitLocker is a feature for protecting against unauthorized access to local drive data, including data stored on fixed or removable drives. When a drive is encrypted with BitLocker, the drive can only be unlocked with a password or a smart card credential. In the case where all unlock methods become unsuccessful, you must use a recovery key to regain access to the drive.

BitLocker supports fixed data drive when the drive is formatted with exFAT, FAT16, FAT32, or NTFS and that there is 64 MB of available disk space. To allow the drive to be unlocked automatically by the operating system for normal usage, the operating system drive itself must be protected by BitLocker. Keep in mind, if you want to encrypt the operating system drive, there are special requirements to meet. BitLocker stores its own encryption and decryption key in a hardware device separate from your hard disk so you must have either a computer with a Trusted Platform Module TPM or a removable USB storage device.

Note that for a TPM to be used by BitLocker, it must have a RSA key pair as the endorsement key. Also, the computer must have been configured with a separate active partition to be used as the system partition. To be precise, for BitLocker to operate correctly on operating system drives, you need to have two NTFS partitions, with one for the operating system and another for the system. The system partition needs at least 100 MB for BitLocker. If Windows RE is also there, you need at least 300 MB. This system partition will always remain unencrypted so your computer can start. The partition that holds the operating system can be separately encrypted.

Bitlocker is NOT installed by default so you must add it yourself.

Questions:

1. What is network location?

2. Network Location and Windows Firewall are in theory mutually dependent. True?

3. Encryption for File Sharing Connections can be set to _____-bit encryption for the best possible protection.

4. Compare ISATAP with 6to4.

5. IP-HTTPS permits IPv6 to be tunneled using:

6. Which ipconfig option can delete the DNS name cache?

7. Which ipconfig option can refresh all DHCP leases and even re-register the DNS names?

8. Which ipconfig option can show the contents of the DNS resolver cache?

9. Windows Firewall can be configured via what tool or interface?

10. At the netsh advfirewall context, what command allows you to change to the Netsh AdvFirewall Firewall context?

11. The possible commands in the firewall context include:

12. With Windows Firewall, what are the directions of traffic and the possible actions to take?

13. What is the Windows Service Hardening rule?

14. What are connection security rules for?

15. If you want to perform remote server management from Windows 7, what tool should you use?

16. Describe Server Manager.

17. DirectAccess makes use of _____ for authentication.

18. DirectAccess makes use of _____ for encryption of communications across the Internet.

19. A major requirement for DirectAccess to work is that IPv6 must be implemented. True?

20. BitLocker supports fixed data drive when the drive is formatted with:

21. In a Windows domain, which port is required for Remote Assistance to work?

22. Remote Assistance requires a password of what length?

23. BranchCache can be deployed in a domain-based or non-domain based environment as long as what connection is available?

24. You should not run DHCP service or DHCP Relay Agent with NAT addressing enabled due to what reason?

25. You should NOT use DHCP to configure a VPN server. Instead you should:

26. The RRAS Packet Filter is configurable through:

Answers:

1. *Network location is a profile containing a collection of network and sharing settings which can be applied to the network you are connected to.*

2. *Network Location and Windows Firewall are in theory mutually independent.*

3. *Encryption for File Sharing Connections can be set to 128-bit encryption or the weaker 40/56 bit encryption.*

4. *ISATAP allows unicast communication between IPv6/IPv4 hosts across your IPv4 intranet. 6to4 allows unicast communication to take place between IPv6/IPv4 hosts and IPv6-capable sites through the Internet.*

5. *IP-HTTPS permits IPv6 to be tunneled using HTTP with SSL as a transport.*

6. */flushdns is an option that can delete the DNS name cache.*

7. */registerdns is an option that can refresh all DHCP leases and even re-register the DNS names.*

8. */displaydns is an option that can show the contents of the DNS resolver cache.*

9. *Windows Firewall can now be configured via the Windows Firewall with Advanced Security MMC snap-in or the Netsh advfirewall command.*

10. *At the netsh advfirewall context, the firewall command allows you to change to the Netsh AdvFirewall Firewall context so you can view, create, and modify firewall rules.*

11. *The possible commands are add, delete, set and show.*

12. *Direction of traffic is either in or out, while action can be allow, block or bypass.*

13. *The Windows Service Hardening rule can restrict services from establishing connections in ways not intended out of the box.*

14. *Connection security rules define authentication using IPsec and enforce Network Access Protection NAP policy.*

15. *If you want to perform remote server management from Windows 7, you use the Remote Server Administration Tools RSAT.*

16. *A very useful tool is the Server Manager. When you are a member of the Administrators group, you can manage roles and features on server computer running either the full or Server Core installation options of Server 2008 R2.*

17. *DirectAccess makes use of IPsec for authentication.*

18. *DirectAccess makes use of IPsec for encryption of communications across the Internet.*

19. *A major requirement for DirectAccess to work is that IPv6 must be implemented.*

20. *BitLocker supports fixed data drive when the drive is formatted with exFAT, FAT16, FAT32, or NTFS and that there is 64 MB of available disk space.*

21. *In a Windows domain, you can enable the Windows Firewall exception for Remote Assistance so Port 135 TCP can be made open for Remote Assistance to work.*

22. *The Remote Assistance Wizard can actually create an email or file invitation for remote assistance and also generate a password (an automatically-generated 12-character password) for the necessary session.*

23. *BranchCache can be deployed in a domain-based or non-domain based environment, as long as a VPN or DirectAccess connection is available between the content servers and the branch office.*

24. *RRAS supports NAT. HOWEVER, since NAT already includes addressing and name resolution features that provide DHCP and DNS services to clients, you should not run DHCP service or DHCP Relay Agent with NAT addressing enabled.*

25. *You should NOT use DHCP to configure a VPN server. It is recommended that you manually configure TCP/IP or use DHCP with MAC address reservations so that the TCP/IP configuration of the VPN server can be kept stable.*

26. *The RRAS Packet Filter is a stateless mechanism. It is configurable through the RRAS MMC snap-in, the netsh based scripting mechanism or the remote access policies.*

Security Threats

Malware

Malware is software designed to infiltrate or damage a computer system without the owner's informed consent. It is a blend of the words "malicious" and "software". The expression is a general term used by computer professionals to mean a variety of forms of hostile, intrusive, or annoying software or program code. Software is considered malware based on the intent of the creator rather than any particular features. It includes computer viruses, worms, trojan horses, spyware, adware, and other unwanted software, which are quite often spread through email attachments. Some newest malware uses web site scripting languages like Javascript and Active X to carry malicious code, which could be easily downloaded through a Web browser and executed in a totally unnoticed way. Newer browsers do allow you to configure and restrict such functionalities.

Viruses and worms

The best-known types of malware are viruses and worms, which are known for the manner in which they spread, rather than any other particular behavior. Originally, the term computer virus was used for a program which infected other executable software, while a worm transmitted itself over a network to infect computers. More recently, the words are often used interchangeably.

NOTE: Just because you have antivirus software installed on your PC doesn't guarantee you are protected against the latest malware threats. To maintain your protection, you have to use the latest version of antivirus software available for your PC. You should also update the virus definitions daily with the LiveUpdate utility that comes with your antivirus software.

Spyware

Spyware applications are typically bundled as a hidden component of freeware or shareware programs that can be downloaded from the Internet. Once installed, the spyware monitors user activity on the Internet and transmits that information in the background to someone else. Since spyware is using memory and system resources for its own purpose at the background, it can lead to system crashes or general system instability.

Trojan horse

As a common type of Trojan horses, a legitimate software might have been corrupted with malicious code which runs when the program is used. The key is that the user has to invoke the program in order to trigger the malicious code. In other words, a trojan horse simply cannot operate autonomously. You would also want to know that most but not all trojan horse payloads are harmful - a few of them are harmless.

Most trojan horse programs are spread through e-mails. Some earlier trojan horse programs were bundled in "Root Kits". For example, the Linux Root Kit version 3 (lrk3) which was released in December 96 had tcp wrapper trojans included and enhanced in the kit.

Keystroke logger

Keystroke logging (in the form of spyware) was originally a function of diagnostic tool deployed by software developers for capturing user's keystrokes. This is done for determining the sources of error or for measuring staff productivity. Imagine if someone uses it to capture user input of critical business data such as CC info ... You may want to use anti spyware applications to detect and clean them up. Web-based on-screen keyboards may be a viable option for web applications.

Keystroke Monitoring is a formal security process whereby administrators view and record the keystrokes entered by the user and the computer's immediate response. Keystroke Monitoring has to rely on keystroke logger to function though.

Software Flaws

Computer code is regarded by some as just a form of mathematics. It is theoretically possible to prove the correctness of computer programs though the likelihood of actually achieving this in large-scale practical systems is regarded as unlikely in the extreme by most with practical experience in the industry. In practice, only a small fraction of computer program code is mathematically proven, or even goes through comprehensive information technology audits or inexpensive but extremely valuable computer security audits.

Software flaws such as buffer overflows, are often exploited to gain control of a computer, or to cause it to operate in an unexpected manner. Buffer overflow (buffer overrun) is supposed to be a programming error which may result in memory access exception - that is, a process make attempt to store data beyond the fixed boundaries of a buffer area. With careless programming, this kind of access attempt can be triggered by ill-intended codes. Stack-based buffer overflows and heap-based buffer overflows are the 2 popular types of attack of this nature. Techniques such as Static code analysis can help preventing such attack. You should also always opt for the use of safe libraries.

Many development methodologies rely on testing to ensure the quality of any code released; this process often fails to discover extremely unusual potential exploits. The term "exploit" generally refers to small programs designed to take advantage of a software flaw that has been discovered, either remote or local.

Sniffing, Eavesdropping and Footprinting

As a pre-attack activity, footprinting refers to the technique of collecting information about systems thru techniques such as Ping Sweeps, TCP Scans, OS Identification, Domain Queries and DNS Interrogation. Tools involved may include samspade, nslookup, traceroute, neotrace and the like. Passive fingerprinting, on the other hand, is based primarily on sniffer traces from your remote system. Rather than proactively querying a remote system, you capture packets that pass-by instead. Passive fingerprinting is very difficult to detect.

Any data that is transmitted over an IP network is at some risk of being eavesdropped or even modified. Voice over IP has the same security issues as running regular applications which rely on IP for transmission.

Non-IP based networks are also highly hack-able. Sniffing was pretty common on the Ethernet (and also on IP networks). Packet sniffer (another name for protocol analyzer) can be deployed to intercept and log netowrk traffic that passes through the network. It can capture unicast, multicast and broadcast traffic provided that you put your network adapter into promiscuous mode. You may sniff to analyze network problems, or to gain information for launching a network attack.

Wireshark (formerly Ethereal) is a free protocol analyzer you may use for network troubleshooting and sniffing. The functionality it offers is similar to tcpdump but it provides a GUI for ease of use.

Even machines that operate as a closed system can be eavesdropped upon via monitoring the faint electro-magnetic transmissions generated by the hardware such as TEMPEST.

DoS and DDoS

A computer system is no more secure than the human systems responsible for its operation. Malicious individuals have regularly penetrated well-designed, secure computer systems by taking advantage of the carelessness of trusted individuals, or by deliberately deceiving them. The availability of the internet makes penetration even easier as everything is now connected. *Attacking web servers had become an exciting yet enjoyable challenge by hackers.*

Denial of service (DoS) attacks are not primarily a means to gain unauthorized access or control of a system. They are instead designed to render it unusable. Attackers can deny service to individual victims, such as by deliberately guessing a wrong password 3 consecutive time and thus causing the victim account to be locked, or they may overload the capabilities of a machine or network and block all users altogether. These types of attack are, in practice, very hard to prevent, because the behavior of whole networks needs to be analyzed, not only of small pieces of code.

Distributed denial of service (DDoS) is even worse - a large number of compromised hosts are used to flood a target system with network requests, thus attempting to render it unusable through resource exhaustion.

Social Engineering

Social engineering is a collection of techniques used to manipulate people into performing actions or divulging confidential information. While similar to a confidence trick or simple fraud, the term typically applies to trickery for information gathering or computer system access.

Technically speaking, all Social Engineering techniques are based on flaws in human logic known as cognitive biases. These bias flaws are used in various combinations to create attack techniques. For example, pretexting is the act of creating and using an invented scenario (the pretext) to persuade a target to release information or perform an action and is usually done over the telephone. It's more than a simple lie as it most often involves some prior research or set up and the use of pieces of known information to establish legitimacy in the mind of the target.

Phishing, on the other hand, applies to email appearing to come from a legitimate business requesting "verification" of information and warning of some dire consequence if it is not done. Sadly, social engineering and direct computer access attacks can only be effectively prevented by non-computer means, which can be difficult to enforce, relative to the sensitivity of the information. Social engineering attacks in particular are very difficult to foresee and prevent.

Identity theft

Identity theft occurs when someone uses another individual's personal information to take on that person's identity. This act could be much more than misuse of a name and a Social Security number as it often deals with fraudulent credit card use and mail fraud. Identity theft can become extremely easy when one's computer is being hacked into. That's why personal firewall should be used on desktop for home use.

Backdoors and rootkits

Many computer manufacturers used to preinstall backdoors on their systems to provide technical support for customers. With the existences of backdoors, it is possible to bypass normal authentication while intended to remain hidden to casual inspection. The backdoor may take the form of an installed program or could be in the form of an existing "legitimate" program, or executable file.

A backdoor refers to a generally undocumented means of getting into a system, mostly for programming and maintenance/troubleshooting needs. Most real world programs have backdoors.

On Windows some backdoor programs may get themselves installed to start when the system boots. You want to know if there are services that are somewhat configured to automatically start - they may be Trojan horse or backdoor program. A specific form of backdoors is rootkit, which replaces system binaries of the operating system to hide the presence of other programs, users, services and open ports. rootkit originally describes those recompiled Unix tools that would hide any trace of the intruder. You can say that the only purpose of rootkit is to hide evidence from system administrators so there is no way to detect malicious special privilege access attempts.

To some, secrecy means security so closed source software solutions are preferable. In the modern days this may not always be true. With the open source model, people may freely revise and inspect codes so back doors and other hidden tricks / defects can hardly go undetected.

Direct access attacks may be conducted through the use of common consumer devices. For example, someone gaining physical access to a computer can install all manner of devices to compromise security, including operating system modifications, software worms, keyboard loggers, and covert listening devices. The attacker can also easily download large quantities of data onto backup media or portable devices.

Other vulnerabilities

You may think of salami attack as a concept that can be applied to scenarios with and without relation to computing. In general, a salami attack is said to have taken place when tiny amounts of assets are systematically acquired from a very large number of sources. Since the process takes place below the threshold of perception and detection, an ongoing accumulation of assets bit by bit is made possible. An example: the digits representing currency on a financial institution's computer could be modified in such a way that values to the right of the pennies field are automatically rounded down. The salami concept can apply in information gathering - aggregating small amounts of information from many sources with an attempt to derive an overall picture of an organization.

Bribes and extortion can occur! With promises or threats that cause your staff to violate their trust, information security can be at risk big time! This is more a HR issue but still you need to think of ways to safeguard security assuming bribery is not entirely impossible.

P3P

The Platform for Privacy Preferences Project (P3P) is a W3C effort which enables web sites to express their privacy practices in a standard format that can be retrieved automatically and interpreted easily by the various user agent software. Agent software are supposed to be able to automate decision-making based on the P3P practices when appropriate. The goal is to make the privacy/data-gathering process more transparent.

Database Specific Risks

You should create individual database user accounts for each person who will be accessing your database. It is technically possible to share accounts between users, but for accountability and control you should not do this. The methods for creating user accounts vary from platform to platform so you will have to consult your DBMS-specific documentation for the exact procedure. Also remember to regularly audit SQL logins for null or weak passwords.

SQL Injection is kind of like a subset of an unverified user input vulnerability. It basically tries to fool your SQL application into running malicious SQL code on the fly. It is all about the application's internal error-handling procedures. For example, if you enter something weird into a web form field and get a server error rather than a custom made error message form in return, chance is that the error handling routine is not handling problematic input properly and may like be exploited.

If ASP is in use, a HTML page often uses the POST command to send parameters to another ASP page or script. Therefore, by checking the source code of the HTML and looking for the "FORM" tag, from within the action field you can tell the asp script in use as well as the method to use for dealing with the script. Such information could be useful exploit wise.

When the underlying codes are SQL codes which directly handle the user input, and if the user input is a bunch of SQL commands embraced with single quotes or double quotes, there may be a chance for the nesting of SQL codes to happen. In the http://www.securiteam.com site there is an article titled "SQL Injection Walkthrough" which gives a bunch of real life SQL injection examples.

sqlmap is an automatic blind SQL injection tool capable of testing for numeric, single quotes string and double quotes string SQL injection on all url dynamic parameters. Other tools which may automate the actual SQL injection process include SQL Injector (which is part of the WebInspect) and Absinthe.

Wikto is a GUI based Web Server Assessment Tool capable of understanding the Google Hack database and running all tests automatically. It can also be used to perform web server fingerprinting. Google Hack is a Perl package that makes use of the Google API to interact with Google for retriving query results and performing basic Natural Language Processing. Attackers may use it to take advantage of the power of the Google search engine for ferreting out the SQL Server errors.

Blind SQL injection is special in that the attacker does not receive feedback from the Web server in the form of error messages. This kind of attack can be slow due to the guesswork involved. In any case, sanitizing the input and quotesafe-ing the input would usually suffice in preventing this kind of attack from hurting you. Another option would be to use stored procedure instead of SQL for data access and manipulation.

SQL Server may be accessed either through a named pipe or a network protocol like TCP. Even when SQL Server uses only named pipes as its protocol, it may still be accessed from the outside via UDP port 1434. The SQL Server Resolution Service running on UDP port 1434 allows one to find hidden database instances. This port is in fact quite dangerous as buffer overflow may occur when an overly long request is sent to the broadcast address for this port.

SQLPing is a great tool that can be used to identify SQL Server systems and their version numbers. If a target being tested with SQLPing does provide critical server information in return, you must consider blocking its port 1434 immediately.

Concealing hard disk data

Generally speaking, differences can be found between different file systems concerning their deletion mechanisms. Complete data removal is, sadly, quite impossible without physically destroying the disk platter(s) on which it was originally written. The operating system's file management system would generally leave data on the physical storage media when it deletes the data files. Following a logical deletion of a file, the file management system would update its file allocation entries to indicate that the space that was once reserved is now available. During this procedure, the file names contained within the directory structure would be altered such that users would no longer have access to the deleted files. Secure removal is an inherently slow operation, and that deletion of large files would be intolerably slow. Also, file meta-data would never be completely overwritten by the user as user level programs would hardly remove important file meta-data (such as user and group ownership, the number of blocks the file contained, and the deletion time ...etc).

On some OS the data that makes up the file stored on disk would actually remain intact during the deletion operation, that the file locations would simply be moved back to the pool of available disk space that can be written to as needed. Disk wiping identifies the method for overwriting a file until the file is rendered unrecoverable. There are many methods of performing a wiping operation (you may refer to the Department of Defense's U.S. DoD 5200.28-STD and the Peter Gutmann scheme). These techniques would normally overwrite a file a specified number of times using a particular pattern or procedure believed to be effective in altering the magnetic structure of the data. HOWEVER, even if a tool was able to completely wipe a drive, some techniques could still provide the ability to retrieve data from media that has been completely overwritten.

The concept of data destruction through an overwriting scheme is similar to the basic idea of degaussing. It is about flipping the magnetic domains on the disk back and forth as much as possible while trying to avoid writing a duplicate pattern twice in a row. For degaussing to be successful, the source would need to be quite powerful - for example, a magnetic force of five times greater than the coercivity of the medium might be required for sufficiently destroying the data.

Review Questions:

1. Most trojan horse programs are spread through:

2. What are the best-known types of malware?

3. How does NAT perform address translation?

4. What is a key escrow system?

5. How does SQL injection work? What about blind SQL injection?

6. Describe salami attack.

7. What is disk wiping all about?

8. What tool can you use to identify SQL Server systems and their version numbers?

9. Phishing applies primarily to:

10. Why is it that the concept of data destruction through an overwriting scheme is similar to the basic idea of degaussing?

Answers:

1. *Most trojan horse programs are spread through e-mails. Some earlier trojan horse programs were bundled in "Root Kits".*

2. *The best-known types of malware are viruses and worms, which are known for the manner in which they spread, rather than any other particular behavior.*

3. *Some firewall and proxy software can perform Network Address Translation (NAT), which allows a LAN to use one set of IP addresses for internal traffic and a second set of addresses for external traffic.*

4. *A key escrow system describes a system which entrusts the two components comprising a cryptographic key (i.e. the two values from which a key can be derived) to two key component holders (who are the escrow agents).*

5. *SQL Injection is kind of like a subset of an unverified user input vulnerability. It basically tries to fool your SQL application into running malicious SQL code on the fly. Blind SQL injection is special in that the attacker does not receive feedback from the Web server in the form of error messages. This kind of attack can be slow due to the guesswork involved.*

6. *You may think of salami attack as a concept that can be applied to scenarios with and without relation to computing. In general, a salami attack is said to have taken place when tiny amounts of assets are systematically acquired from a very large number of sources.*

7. *Disk wiping identifies the method for overwriting a file until the file is rendered unrecoverable. There are many methods of performing a wiping operation.*

8. *SQLPing is a great tool that can be used to identify SQL Server systems and their version numbers.*

9. *Phishing applies to email appearing to come from a legitimate business requesting "verification" of information and warning of some dire consequence if it is not done.*

10. *The concept of data destruction through an overwriting scheme is similar to the basic idea of degaussing. It is about flipping the magnetic domains on the disk back and forth as much as possible while trying to avoid writing a duplicate pattern twice in a row.*

System Monitoring

Event Viewer

Event logging starts automatically when you start Windows Server 2008 R2. You can find Event Viewer via Computer Management or Server Manager:

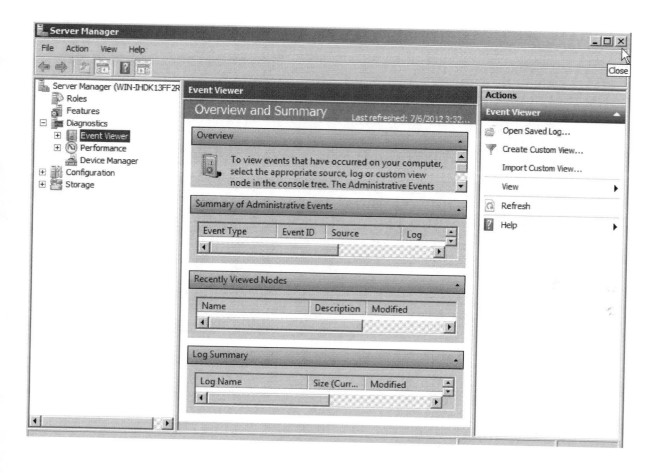

There are different types of application or program events. Hardware events are also under this category. Officially, the types of Applications and Services logs include are Admin, which record problems that directly affect end users;

Operational, which may not always indicate problems but simply records of event occurrences; Analytic, which deals with specialized issues with Windows; Debug, which gives records of problems for programmers to solve problems; and Internet Explorer.

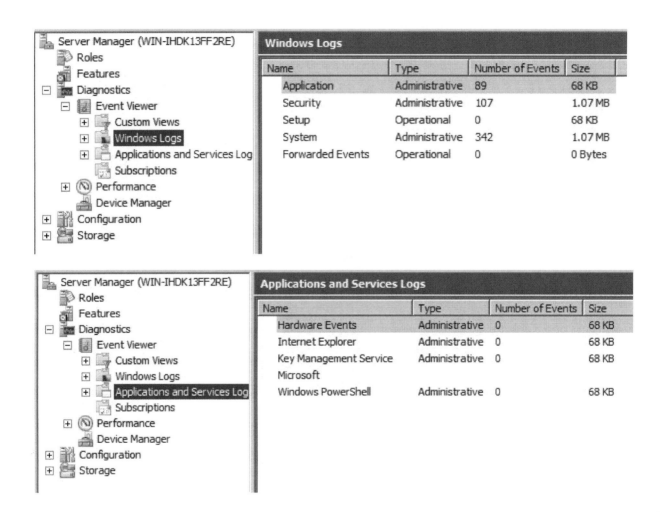

Application or program events are further classified into error, warning, and information depending on their seriousness. An error describes a significant problem. A warning is not yet a significant problem but is likely a problem soon. An information event simply describes successful operation.

Security-related events are audits that describe success or failure of an event. Setup events are for reviewing actions occurred during Windows Setup and the performance statistics for different parts of Windows Setup. The log file is called Setup.etl. System events are logged by Windows and Windows system services. They may be error, warning, or information. Forwarded events are those that have been forwarded to here by other computers on the network. Setup log deals with application setup. Because events logged are saved in XML format, it is technically possible to construct XML queries to parse the output for display in somewhere else. Do note that it is possible to change the log size and the overwrite behaviors of log entries. Also note that it is possible to collect copies of events from multiple remote computers. To precisely specify the remote to collect, you create an event subscription.

You may use Event Viewer to troubleshoot a problem by locating all events that are related regardless of which event log they appear in. You do this by creating a custom view which can filter for specific events across multiple logs. In Event Viewer, you may choose Action - Create Custom View to achieve this. It is important for you to control the size of the logs due to the risk of running out of log storage space. You may specify the max log size and what to do if the max size is reached. The possible log retention policies are:

- Overwrite events as needed, meaning new events are continue to be stored when the log file is full, and that each new incoming event will replace the oldest event in the log.

- Archive the log when full without overwriting any events.

- Do not overwrite any events so you must clear the logs manually. You can clear events via the Event Viewer or the wevtutil command line command.

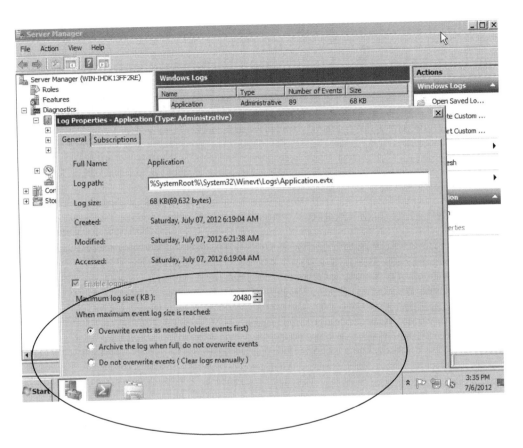

Subscription is all about collecting events from other computers. The Event Collector Service must be made running. Before creating a subscription to collect events on a computer, there is a need to first configure both the collecting computer and the computer from which events will be collected. You need to run the winrm quickconfig command on the source computer. You then need to use the wecutil qc command on the collector computer. Finally you need to add the computer account of the collector computer to the local Administrators group of the source computer.

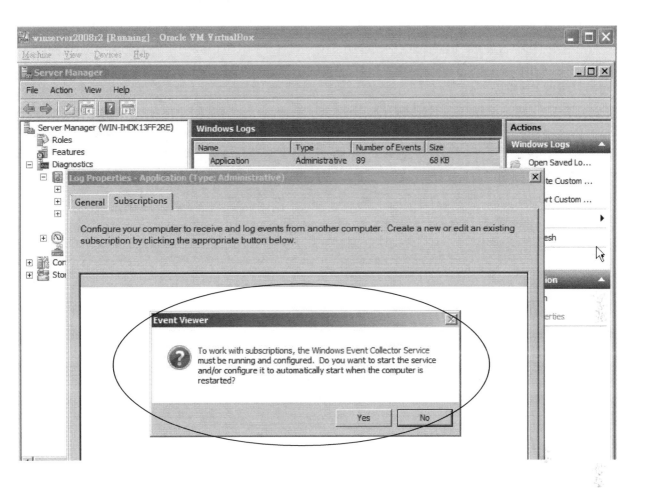

There are different Event Delivery Optimization Options. The Normal option ensures reliable delivery of events without making any attempt to conserve bandwidth. The Minimize Bandwidth option strictly control the use of network bandwidth for event delivery. It makes use of push delivery with a batch timeout of 6 hours. Minimize Latency focuses on event delivery with minimal delay. The batch timeout is set to 30 seconds.

Resource Monitoring

Resource Monitor provides real time information on CPU, disk, network, and memory usage. You have to be a member of the local Administrators group or equivalent in order to use Resource Monitor. If you see constantly high utilization in a particular area, further investigation may be necessary.

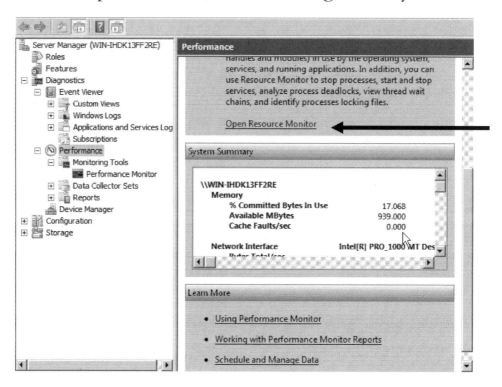

You can actually use Resource Monitor to monitor I/O performance at the file level. Information on reads, writes, and response time for individual files are all available. You want to know that Response Time in milliseconds should be kept low - anything less than 10 ms is considered good.

Review Questions:

1. Event logging starts automatically when you start Windows Server. True?

2. Only administrators can view the security logs. True?

3. Application or program events are classified into error, warning, and ...

4. Compare warning with error.

5. What are security-related events?

6. Setup event log file has the name of:

7. Events logged are saved in what format?

8. Resource Monitor provides real time information on:

Answers:

1. *Event logging starts automatically when you start Windows Server.*

2. *Only administrators can view the security logs.*

3. *Application or program events are classified into error, warning, and information depending on their seriousness.*

4. *An error describes a significant problem. A warning is not yet a significant problem but is likely a problem soon.*

5. *Security-related events are audits that describe success or failure of an event.*

6. *The log file is called Setup.etl.*

7. *Events logged are saved in XML format.*

8. *Resource Monitor provides real time information on CPU, disk, network, and memory usage.*

User Management

Shared Folders

You can create folder share simply by right clicking on the folder and choose the appropriate sharing option. You can also manage shared folders via Computer Management. The Shares node shows all shared folders on the computer while the Sessions node displays full details on which remote users currently are connected to the shared folders. You can easily edit the properties of a share by right-clicking it and then select properties. You can also create a shared folder by right-clicking the Shares node and then choose New Share for invoking the Create a Shared Folder Wizard.

An alternative to using the GUI is to use the net share command. You can use net share to create, configure and delete network shares from the command line. The /grant switch specifies the access rights granted, while /users specifies the max number of users who can access the share. As a user of a shared resource, one can use net use to connect to or disconnect from a shared resource, or displays information about the available computer connections. Resource must be specified in this format - \\ ComputerName \ ShareName. You can use /user to specify a different user name with which the connection is being made. You can also use /savecred to store the provided credentials for easy reuse.

Users and Groups

Local users and groups can be managed through the Server Manager. You can create, modify or remove users and groups as needed.

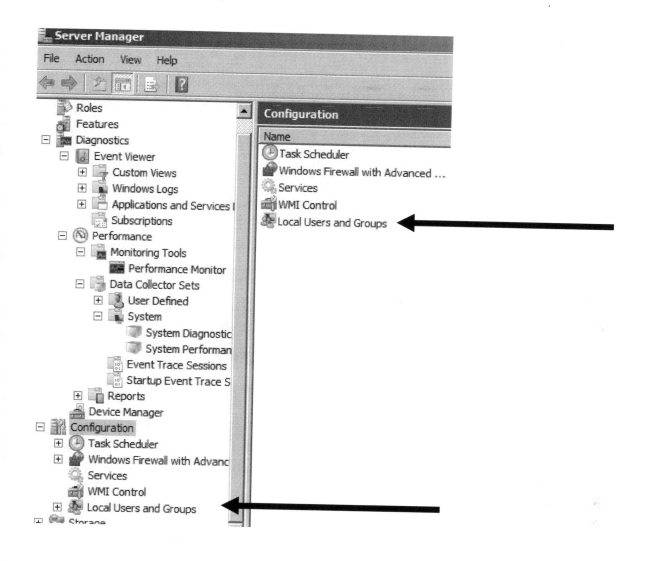

The two default user accounts are Administrator and Guest. A bunch of default groups are also in there. The Administrator account cannot be deleted. You also cannot have it removed from the Administrators group. However, you may have it renamed or disabled. Renaming it to something else can make hacking more difficult. Do keep in mind, even when the Administrator account is disabled, it can still be used for access through Safe Mode. In fact one can use the System Configuration tool (msconfig) to restart in Safe Mode. One can also boot into Safe Mode by pressing the **"F8"** key just before the Windows boot screen appears.

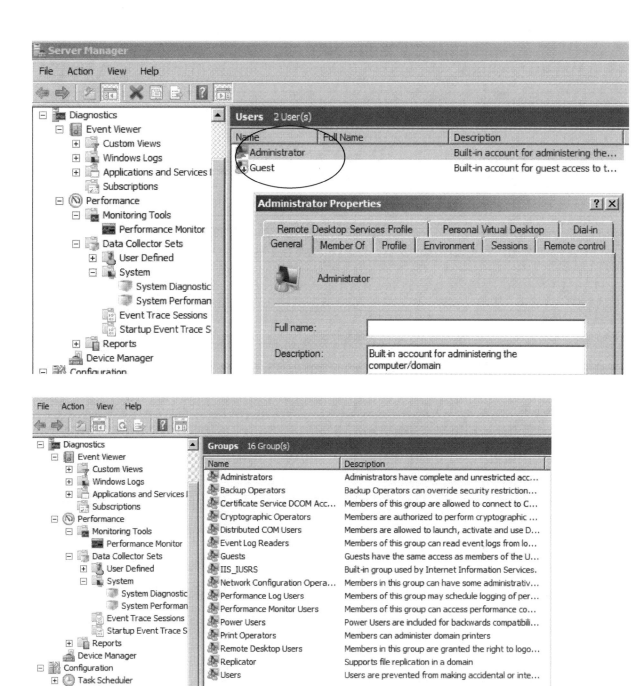

The Groups folder shows the default local groups as well as the local groups that you have created. You should limit the number of users in the

Administrators group since these people have Full Control permissions on the local computer. Unless strictly necessary, you should leave the Guest account disabled. This Guest account is dangerous since it does not require a password, but it is disabled by default anyway. Do note that some default user rights that are assigned to certain default local groups may actually allow members of those groups to exercise additional admin rights on the local computer, so you should equally trust all personnel that are members of the Administrators and Backup Operators groups.

IIS_IUSRS is a built-in group used only by IIS. Network Configuration Operators can make changes to TCP/IP settings. Performance Log Users can manage performance counters, logs, and alerts locally and from remote clients. Performance Monitor Users can monitor performance counters locally and from remote clients.

Power Users is a legacy feature. Remote Desktop Users can log on to the computer remotely. Replicator is for logging onto the Replicator services of a domain controller and should not be used to accommodate user accounts of actual users. Backup Operators can back up and restore files regardless of any permission that protect those files but they cannot change any of the related security settings.

Local users are NOT the same as domain users. Domain users have their accounts stored in AD, not just locally. Domain admins can perform tasks that involved AD. Local admins can only perform admin tasks on the local machine.

Questions:

1. What are the two default user accounts?

2. The Administrator account cannot be deleted. However, you can have it removed from the Administrators group. True?

3. _____ is a built-in group used only by IIS.

4. Describe the Replicator group.

5. Describe the Backup Operators group.

Answers:

1. *The two default user accounts are Administrator and Guest.*

2. *The Administrator account cannot be deleted. You also cannot have it removed from the Administrators group. However, you may have it renamed or disabled.*

3. *IIS_IUSRS is a built-in group used only by IIS.*

4. *Replicator is for logging onto the Replicator services of a domain controller and should not be used to accommodate user accounts of actual users.*

5. *Backup Operators can back up and restore files regardless of any permission that protect those files but they cannot change any of the related security settings.*

Configuring DNS, DHCP and WINS

Naming guidelines

A DNS name has at least two parts separated by periods. The rightmost is the top-level domain while the other parts are subdomains, which usually refer to the owner organization. When creating DNS names for internal computers, it is recommended that you follow a logical computer-naming convention so that users can remember the names easily.

You may want to match the AD domain name to the primary DNS suffix of the computer name, which is the part of the name that shows up after the host name. You should not assign the same computer name to different computers in different DNS domains even though technically it is possible to do so. Use only ASCII characters but not symbols or hyphen to ensure interoperability with older computers.

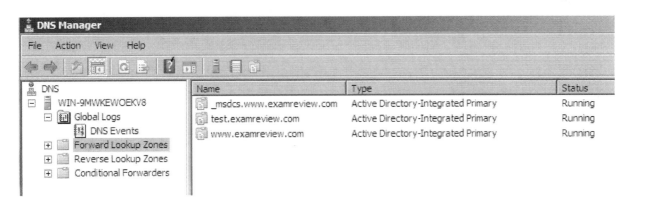

The DNS Manager

Assuming you are part of the AD, you may use the DNS Manager to configure DNS settings. When creating a new domain and/or forest, the Active Directory Domain Services Installation Wizard will install the DNS server role by default since DNS and AD DS need to have proper integration in order to work as expected. The IP address of the DNS server should be static so that clients can locate it reliably. This is NOT a "technical MUST" but a highly recommended setting.

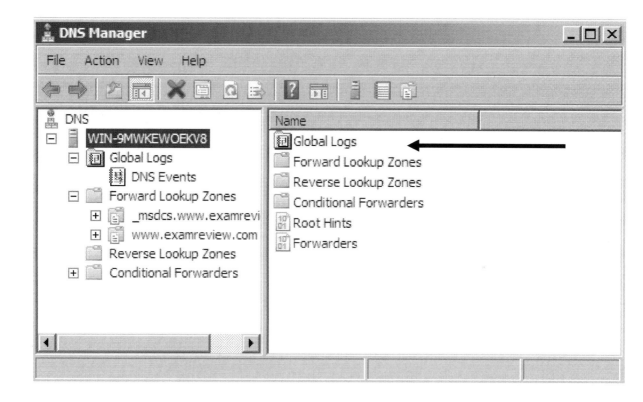

DNS clients typically need a forward lookup which expects to receive an IP address as the resource data for the query response. A reverse lookup process is the opposite - the IP addresses are known and they look for the corresponding DNS names. A special domain known as in-addr.arpa was defined in the DNS standards for providing a practical way to perform reverse queries.

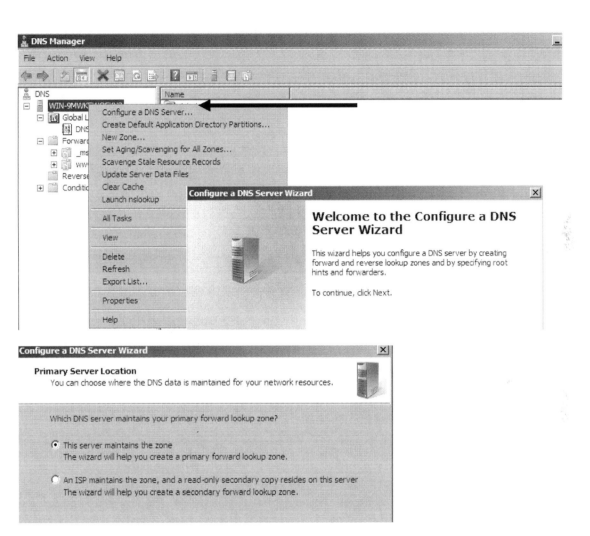

A DNS namespace may be divided into zones for storing name information of one or more DNS domains. A zone often serves as the authoritative source for information of a domain. It is popular to use a zone to represent a domain, and "delegate away" to another zone for representing a sub domain.

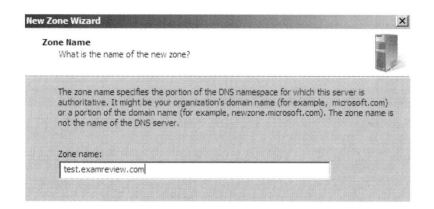

When the Active Directory Domain Services Installation Wizard configures DNS on a new domain controller, it will create resource records necessary for the proper operation of the DNS server. You should not touch these records or you may get things corrupted.

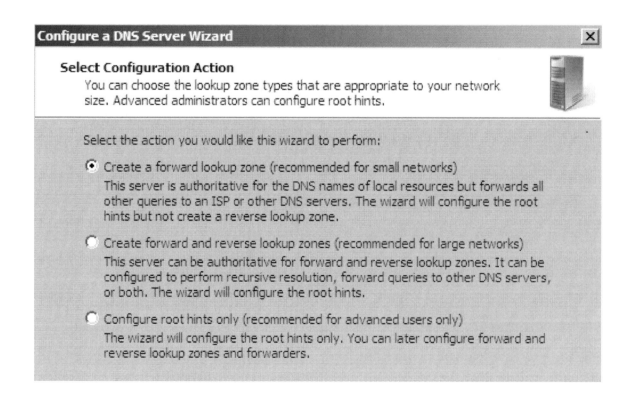

If you configure a new forest AFTER configuring DNS, the zone used by your organization is already in the Forward Lookup Zones section. You may still right click on the server and choose Configure a DNS Server to create a new zone. A host (A) resource record is for associating the DNS domain name of a computer to an IP address. You only need to have such a resource record for computer that shares resources on the network that needs to be identified by the DNS domain name.

Windows 2000, Windows XP, and Windows Server 2003 clients and servers use DHCP Client service to dynamically register and update their host (A) resource records. Windows Vista, Windows 7/8 and Windows Server 2008 clients use the DNS Client service to achieve the same. So in theory there is no need to manually configure the records unless static configuration is needed somewhere. You can in fact manually create a host (A) resource record for a static TCP/IP client computer.

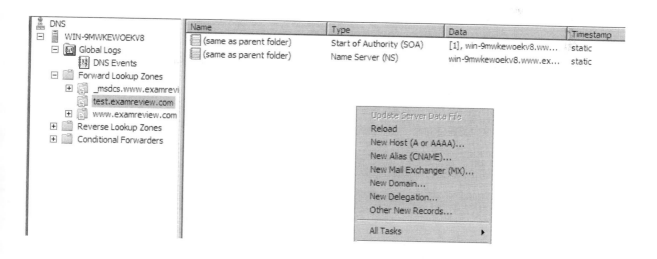

A DHCP server may enable dynamic updates in the DNS namespace for compatible clients. In other words, you may use the DHCP server to register and update the PTR and A resource records on behalf of its clients. To achieve this, the Client FQDN option which is option 81 needs to be configured to allow a client to send its fully qualified domain name FQDN to the DHCP server via the DHCPREQUEST packet. There is a security concern - what if the update request is problematic? With Windows Server 2008, DNS update security can be used for zones that are AD integrated - it is possible to use ACL within the DNS console to add or to remove users or groups from the ACL for certain zones or records.

New Zone Wizard

Dynamic Update
You can specify that this DNS zone accepts secure, nonsecure, or no dynamic updates.

Dynamic updates enable DNS client computers to register and dynamically update their resource records with a DNS server whenever changes occur.

Select the type of dynamic updates you want to allow:

⦿ Allow only secure dynamic updates (recommended for Active Directory)
This option is available only for Active Directory-integrated zones.

○ Allow both nonsecure and secure dynamic updates
Dynamic updates of resource records are accepted from any client.
⚠ This option is a significant security vulnerability because updates can be accepted from untrusted sources.

○ Do not allow dynamic updates
Dynamic updates of resource records are not accepted by this zone. You must update these records manually.

You may have your DNS server designated as a forwarder when the other DNS servers are configured to forward the queries that can't be resolved locally. You can use the DNS Manager or the dnscmd command with the /ResetForwarders option to configure this. You can specify that the DNS server only uses forwarders and not attempt any further recursion should the forwarders fail by selecting the Do not use recursion for this domain check box. You may even choose to disable recursion for the DNS server so that it will never perform recursion on any query, however by doing so you will not be able to use forwarders on the same server anymore. Also, you are not allowed to use a domain name in a conditional forwarder if this DNS server is hosting a primary zone, secondary zone, or stub zone for that domain name.

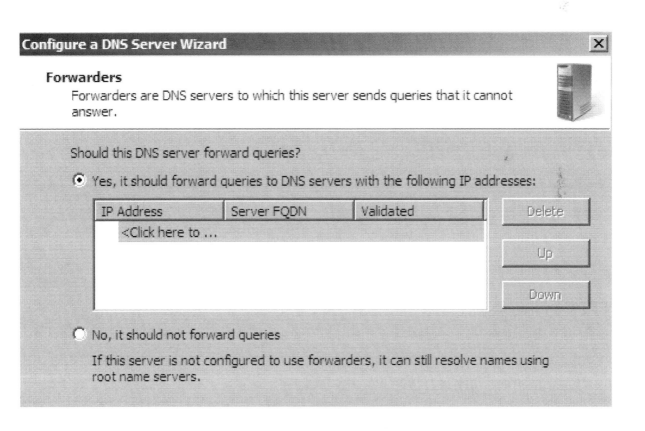

DHCP can register host (A) and pointer (PTR) resource records automatically but older resource records don't go away unless you configure scavenging. with it, the age of a resource record is to be judged based on when it was created or last updated. Normally, Windows computers will send an update request every 24 hours which also serves as sort of a keep alive notice. You may choose to use the option "Enable automatic scavenging of stale records", which is disabled by default. The scavenging intervals of 7-days would usually do fine.

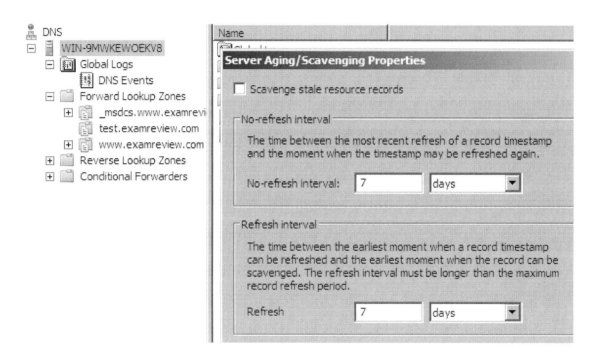

With Windows Server 2008 R2, the DNS Server service will by default try to locate and create a default DNS application directory partitions in Active Directory UNLESS the default DNS application directory partitions are already available. If for whatever reason the DNS Server service fails to do this, you need to manually create the application directory partitions using the DNS console or the dnscmd command with the /CreateBuiltinDirectoryPartitions option.

In a standard DNS zone storage model, name registration updates are performed via a single-master update model with one single authoritative DNS server for a zone designated as the primary source. It maintains the master copy of a zone locally and that any request for an update of zone data would require a full or incremental transfer of the zone database. Simply put, there is only a single point of failure. With AD integrated zone storage, updates to DNS are following a multimaster update model. Any authoritative DNS server (most likely a domain controller running DNS) can act as a primary source. With the master copy of the zone maintained in the Active Directory database and gets fully replicated to all domain controllers, updates can be made at any relevant domain controller - you have redundancy here.

Zone replication scopes determine the amount of replication traffic. You may choose to replicate zone data to:

- all DNS servers in the Active Directory forest

- all DNS servers in the Active Directory domain

- all domain controllers in the Active Directory domain

- all domain controllers in a specified application directory partition

The broader the replication scope the greater the network traffic you will see. Replication does consume bandwidth!

When troubleshooting DNS, you may want to use the ping command via the command line on multiple clients to test resolving the names of hosts both on the intranet and on the Internet, as well as to test overall network connectivity. If you cannot even ping successfully using IP addresses, it is not a DNS issue but a connectivity isue. On the other hand, you may test registration of records for a domain controller via the dcdiag /test:dns /v /s:domain_controller command.

Setting up DHCP and WINS

DHCP is not installed by default so you must add it yourself. Since it is expected to be closely integrated with DNS, you want to have DNS functioning correctly when setting up DHCP.

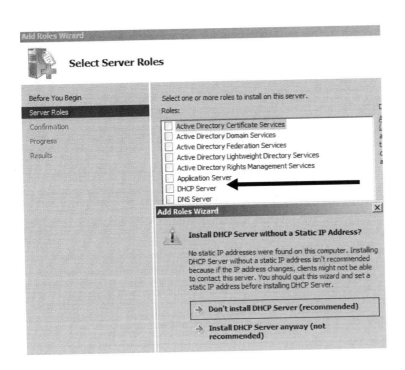

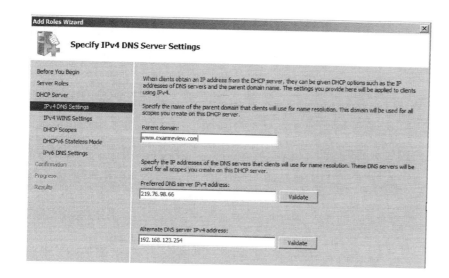

You may specify whether or not WINS is required for supporting older applications that use NetBIOS. You want to remember that Windows 2000, Windows XP, Windows Vista, Windows Server 2003, and Windows Server 2008 can use both DNS names and NetBIOS names. Therefore, unless strictly necessary you may want to go pure DNS and forget about NetBIOS / WINS entirely.

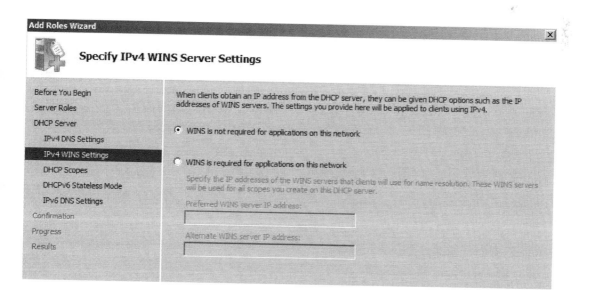

Talking about address scope, you want to set exclusion ranges for any IP addresses within a scope that you do not want the DHCP server to exercise DHCP assignment. Simply put, you use an exclusion range for addresses so to specify that DHCP clients are never offered these addresses. You do this to reserve IP addresses for static assignment, OR to distribute workload among DHCP servers. There is a 80/20 rule for scopes - you want to divide scope addresses between two DHCP servers - one with approximately 80% of the addresses and another with approximately 20% of the addresses. Using multiple DHCP servers for fault tolerance and redundancy is known as split-scope configuration. There is in fact a DHCP Split-Scope Configuration Wizard you can use for IPv4 scopes.

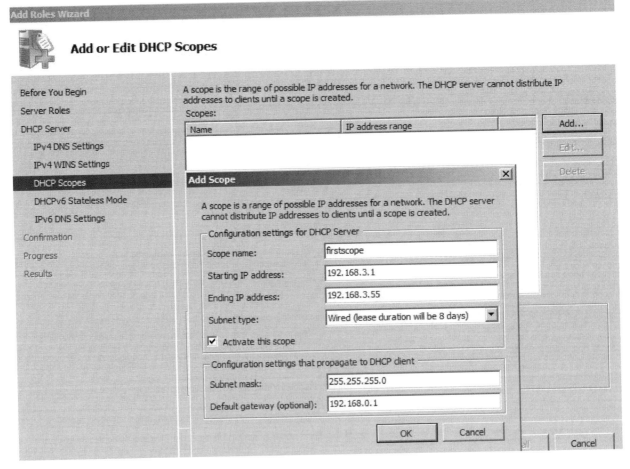

DHCPv6 stateless mode clients may use DHCPv6 to obtain network configuration parameters separately from address configuration. In fact, IPv6 clients may configure an IPv6 address via a non-DHCPv6 based mechanism, including IPv6 address auto-configuration and static configuration. DHCPv6 stateful mode, on the other hand, allows clients to acquire both the IPv6 address and the network configuration parameters through DHCPv6 together.

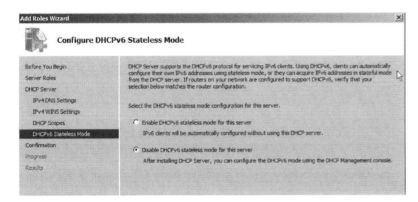

Upon successful configuration, DHCP may be configured via the Server Manager or the DHCP console. Leases may also be viewed and terminated via the DHCP console in real time.

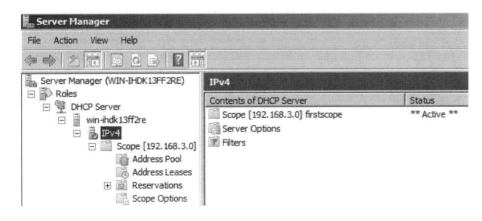

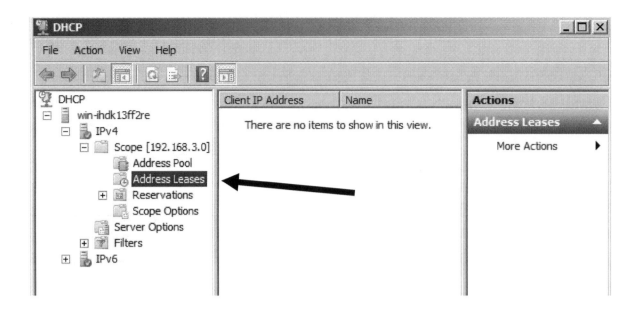

You use a DHCP Relay Agent to relay DHCP messages across different IP networks. DHCP is broadcast-based so you need to help of a relay agent in order to exchange messages with computers on the other side of the router. Because this agent most likely resides on a router, you may enable it via the RRAS console. You may not use it on a computer running DHCP service or NAT routing protocols though. Note that there is also a DHCPv6 Relay Agent that supports similar function for IPv6.

Questions:

1. You should not assign the same computer name to different computers in different DNS domains. True?

2. Why should you use only ASCII characters but not symbols or hyphen in DNS computer names?

3. Describe the reverse lookup process.

4. What is in-addr.arpa?

5. In the DNS namespace, what is a zone for?

6. Why do you need a host (A) resource record?

7. Which Windows versions use the DHCP Client service to dynamically register and update their host (A) resource records?

8. Which Windows versions use the DNS Client service to dynamically register and update their host (A) resource records?

9. How should DHCP option 81 be configured?

10. What is the potential security risk when you use DHCP server to register and update the PTR and A resource records on behalf of its clients?

11. With Windows Server 2008, how does DNS update security work?

12. How do you have your DNS server designated as a forwarder?

13. You are not allowed to use a domain name in a conditional forwarder if:

14. In a standard DNS zone storage model, name registration updates are performed via what model?

15. Describe AD integrated zone storage.

16. What is WINS for?

17. Describe the 80/20 rule for DHCP scopes.

18. Describe split-scope configuration. How do you configure it?

19. Briefly describe the DHCPv6 stateless mode. How is stateful mode different?

20. You use what to relay DHCP messages across different IP networks?

Answers:

1. To avoid confusion you should not assign the same computer name to different computers in different DNS domains even though technically it is possible to do so.

2. Use only ASCII characters but not symbols or hyphen to ensure interoperability with older computers.

3. The IP addresses are known and the clients look for the corresponding DNS names.

4. A special domain known as in-addr.arpa was defined in the DNS standards for providing a practical way to perform reverse queries.

5. A DNS namespace may be divided into zones for storing name information of one or more DNS domains. A zone often serves as the authoritative source for information of a domain.

6. A host (A) resource record is for associating the DNS domain name of a computer to an IP address.

7. Windows 2000, Windows XP, and Windows Server 2003 clients and servers use DHCP Client service to dynamically register and update their host (A) resource records.

8. Windows Vista, Windows 7/8 and Windows Server 2008 clients use the DNS Client service to dynamically register and update their host (A) resource records.

9. The Client FQDN option which is option 81 can be configured to allow a client to send its fully qualified domain name FQDN to the DHCP server via the DHCPREQUEST packet.

10. There is a security concern - what if the update request is problematic?

11. With Windows Server 2008, DNS update security can be used for zones that are AD integrated - it is possible to use ACL within the DNS console to add or to remove users or groups from the ACL for certain zones or records.

12. *You may have your DNS server designated as a forwarder when the other DNS servers are configured to forward the queries that can't be resolved locally. You can use the DNS Manager or the dnscmd command with the /ResetForwarders option to configure this.*

13. *You are not allowed to use a domain name in a conditional forwarder if this DNS server is hosting a primary zone, secondary zone, or stub zone for that domain name.*

14. *In a standard DNS zone storage model, name registration updates are performed via a single-master update model with one single authoritative DNS server for a zone designated as the primary source.*

15. *With AD integrated zone storage, updates to DNS are following a multimaster update model.*

16. *You may specify whether or not WINS is required for supporting older applications that use NetBIOS.*

17. *There is a 80/20 rule for scopes - you want to divide scope addresses between two DHCP servers - one with approximately 80% of the addresses and another with approximately 20% of the addresses.*

18. *Using multiple DHCP servers for fault tolerance and redundancy is known as split-scope configuration. There is in fact a DHCP Split-Scope Configuration Wizard you can use for IPv4 scopes.*

19. *DHCPv6 stateless mode clients may use DHCPv6 to obtain network configuration parameters separately from address configuration. DHCPv6 stateful mode, on the other hand, allows clients to acquire both the IPv6 address and the network configuration parameters through DHCPv6 together.*

20. *You use a DHCP Relay Agent to relay DHCP messages across different IP networks.*

Setting up Certificate Services

Basic Concepts

Cryptography refers to the art and act of protecting information by transforming it into an unreadable format (the cipher text). Once encrypted, only those who possess a secret key can decipher the message back into plain text. Symmetric-key cryptography refers to an encryption system in which the sender and receiver of a message share a single, common key. Public-key cryptology, on the other hand, utilizes two keys, one refers to the public key for encrypting messages and one private key for decrypting them.

With a Public Key Infrastructure PKI, digital certificates rely on public key cryptography. There is a set of components, policies, protocols, and technologies that work together to provide data authentication, integrity, and confidentiality through using certificates, and public and private keys. Data can be protected by applying a hashing algorithm as well as a signature algorithm to the original content.

Symmetric key algorithms use trivially related (or even identical) cryptographic keys for decryption and also encryption. They use much less computational power, but would require the use of a shared secret key on each end. The storage and exchange of such shared secret can be a source of security risk. Asymmetric key algorithms use different keys so they don't have to worry about the shared secret but they consume way more CPU power.

A Certificate Authority CA is an entity that generates and validates digital certificates. It typically adds its own signature to the public key of the client so to indicate that the public key is valid if you trust this CA.

Basic Setup

From Server Manager you need to use the Add Roles Wizard to add Active Directory Certificate Services since it is not installed by default. You do so to configure Certification Authorities CAs. You can use root and subordinate CAs to issue certificates to your users, computers, and services. You can also setup Web enrollment so that users can connect to a CA via Web browser. Online Responder service may be used to implement Online Certificate Status Protocol OCSP - it works by decoding revocation status requests for specific certificates and performing evaluation accordingly. In fact you may use it as an alternative to or an extension of CRLs for providing certificate revocation data to your clients. Do note that the Web edition of Server 2008 R2 does not support any of these.

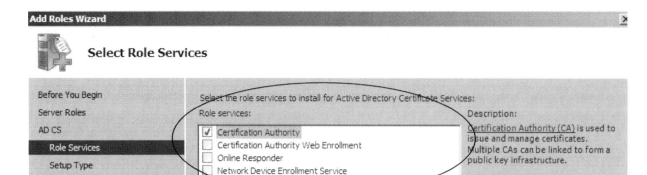

You need to determine the type of CA you prefer. A stand-alone CA does not require the use of AD. When someone sends a certificate request to a stand-alone CA, the requester must manually supply all the identifying information. The necessary authentication information for requests will need to be obtained from the local computer's Security Accounts Manager database. Also, requests will be set to Pending until you the administrator manually verify the identity information. If you choose to use an Enterprise CA, it means the CA is AD integrated so all the manual tasks become automatic UNLESS you are serving people who do not belong to AD. In fact, when a stand-alone CA is installed by a Domain Administrator of the parent domain in an enterprise or by an administrator who has write access to AD, the stand-alone CA will by default publish its CA certificate and revocation list to AD.

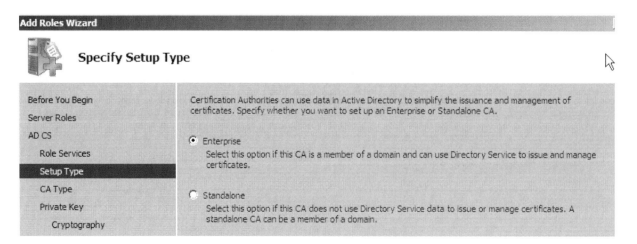

Generally, a standalone CA is better for serving the outside clients while an enterprise one is good for internal use. However, for security concern it is very common to use a third party such as VeriSign as the "external" CA. Inside a network, the first CA installed becomes the root CA, which is in a position to validate all other CAs within the network. A root CA is said to be the most trusted CA in a CA hierarchy. It issues certificates to subordinate CAs. Subordinate CAs may also issue certificates to other subordinate CAs.

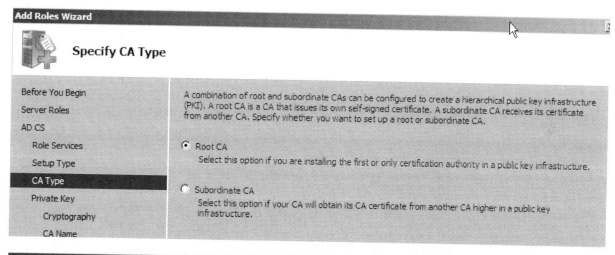

A hash function is often used to turn data into a smaller number which serves as a digital sort of fingerprint. In cryptography, a good hash function allows for "one-way" operation, meaning there is almost no way to calculate the data input value. SHA is one example. It has several variants, which are SHA-1, SHA-224, SHA-256, SHA-384, and SHA-512. They are designed by the NSA and published thru the NIST. MD5 is another example. It uses a 128-bit hash value to create a hash that is typically a 32 character hex number. You need to make a choice here. After this you need to name the CA and specify the duration of the validity of the certificates issued.

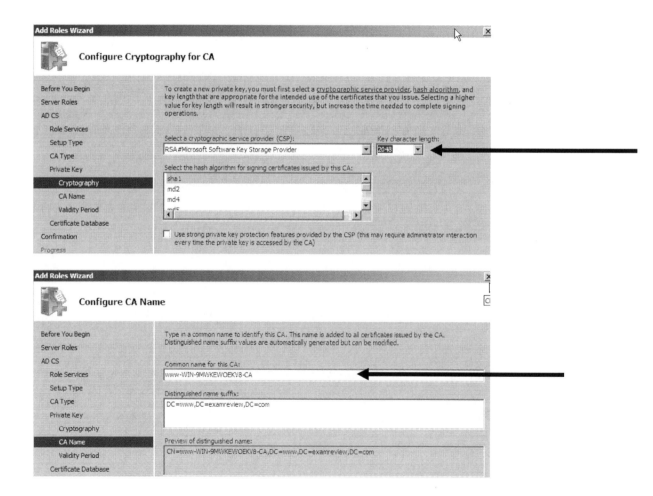

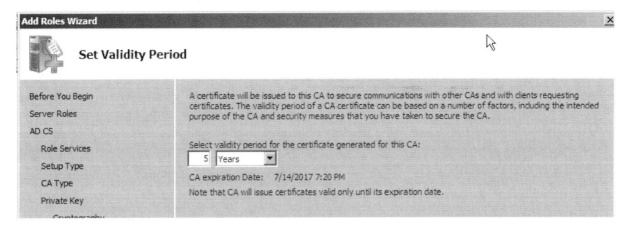

An enterprise CA stores all the certificate information in Active Directory so certificate data can be replicated automatically. Do note that enterprise CAs can only issue certificates to those who are also member of the AD forest. Also, certificate templates that define the format and content of the certificates can only be used with enterprise CAs. A stand-alone CA, in contrast, simply stores its certificate data in a shared folder. There is no need to work with AD. Both can have their own CA hierarchy. When a root CA is installed, you use it to issue CA certificates to other subordinate certificate servers. Management of CAs can be performed via the Certification Authority console.

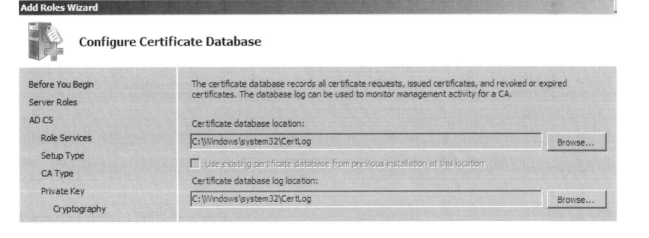

A CA can be maintained locally or via a remote connection. HOWEVER, for the sake of security you want to do it locally. Also note that a Windows 2000 CA may not be managed using the Windows Server 2008 version of the Certification Authority console or vice-versa. You should back up the certification authority database, the CA certificate, and the CA keys on a regular basis given consideration on the number of certificates issued. The more certificates you issue the more frequently the CA should be backed up.

Once you setup a CA on a server, you cannot no longer change the server name and many of the domain settings. If you need to decommission a root CA, make sure all outstanding certificates issued by this CA is revoked. After revocation, a Certificate Revocation List CRL should be published to reflect the change. Apart from the MMC console, a CA can be managed via the certutil command line tool. You may in fact also use certutil to display information on the digital certificates that have been installed on a DirectAccess client, DirectAccess server, or any other intranet resources.

When you renew a root CA, the root CA certificate will have to be re-distributed to all clients that are supposed to trust this root CA. Root CA certificates may also be published manually to AD via certutil.exe with the –dspublish command switch.

Questions:

1. How do you add Active Directory Certificate Services to a server?

2. What is Online Responder service for?

3. The Web edition of Server 2008 R2 does not support the CA role. True?

4. Describe a stand-alone CA in AD.

5. What is going to happen when a stand-alone CA is installed by a Domain Administrator of the parent domain in an enterprise?

6. Generally, a standalone CA is better for serving the outside clients while an enterprise one is good for internal use. True?

7. Which CA is said to be the most trusted CA in a CA hierarchy?

8. How does enterprise CA store its certificate information?

9. Management of CAs can be performed via which GUI?

10. Management of CAs can be performed via which command line tool?

11. Root CA certificates may be published manually to AD via certutil.exe with which command switch?

12. What must be done if you need to decommission a root CA?

13. What must be done if you need to renew a root CA?

Answers:

1. *From Server Manager you need to use the Add Roles Wizard to add Active Directory Certificate Services since it is not installed by default.*

2. *Online Responder service may be used to implement Online Certificate Status Protocol OCSP - it works by decoding revocation status requests for specific certificates and performing evaluation accordingly.*

3. *The Web edition of Server 2008 R2 does not support any feature CA related.*

4. *A stand-alone CA does not require the use of AD. When someone sends a certificate request to a stand-alone CA, the requester must manually supply all the identifying information. Also, requests will be set to Pending until you the administrator manually verify the identity information.*

5. *In fact, when a stand-alone CA is installed by a Domain Administrator of the parent domain in an enterprise or by an administrator who has write access to AD, the stand-alone CA will by default publish its CA certificate and revocation list to AD.*

6. *Generally, a standalone CA is better for serving the outside clients while an enterprise one is good for internal use.*

7. *A root CA is said to be the most trusted CA in a CA hierarchy.*

8. *An enterprise CA stores all the certificate information in Active Directory so certificate data can be replicated automatically.*

9. *Management of CAs can be performed via the Certification Authority console.*

10. *Apart from the MMC console, a CA can be managed via the certutil command line tool.*

11. *Root CA certificates may be published manually to AD via certutil.exe with the – dspublish command switch.*

12. *If you need to decommission a root CA, make sure all outstanding certificates issued by this CA is revoked.*

13. *When you renew a root CA, the root CA certificate will have to be re-distributed to all clients that are supposed to trust this root CA.*

Setting up Active Directory

Basic concepts of AD

Active Directory AD stores information of all network objects and makes the information easy to find. It is a logical and hierarchical presentation and storage of shared resources such as servers, volumes, printers...etc. A global catalog is a domain controller. Every AD has at least one. It stores a copy of all Active Directory objects in a forest. To be precise, it stores a full copy of all objects in the directory for its own domain and a partial copy of all objects for all other domains.

It enables and facilitates user searches for directory information throughout all domains. It also resolves user principal names when the authenticating domain controller doesn't have knowledge of the involved account. And it helps other domain controllers to validate references to those objects that belong to other domains in the forest. The role it plays is very important in the authentication process. If it is not available when a user logs on to a domain, the computer will try to use the cached credentials to log on the user. However, if the user has not logged on before, he will only be able to log on to the local computer.

Installing a domain controller and changing the functional level

You need to install the Active Directory Domain Services AD-DS role on the server so to allow the server to act as a Domain Controller. After this you need to use the dcpromo command to invoke the AD Installation Wizard. If you use the /adv switch you can run the wizard in advanced mode. To perform all the setup tasks, you should be a local admin as well as a domain admin. And you should also have a special restore mode admin password. You will be asked to setup separate password for restore use later.

Add Roles Wizard

Select Server Roles

Before You Begin	Select one or more roles to install on this server.
Server Roles	Roles:
Active Directory Domain Services	☐ Active Directory Certificate Services
Confirmation	☑ Active Directory Domain Services ⬅
Progress	☐ Active Directory Federation Services
Results	☐ Active Directory Lightweight Directory Services
	☐ Active Directory Rights Management Services
	☐ Application Server
	☐ DHCP Server
	☐ DNS Server
	☐ Fax Server

The following roles, role services, or features were installed successfully:

⚠ 1 warning, 1 informational messages below

🛡 Windows automatic updating is not enabled. To install the latest updates, use Windows Update in Control Panel to check for updates.

🔺 **Active Directory Domain Services**   ✅ **Installation succeeded**

The following role services were installed:

Active Directory Domain Controller

ⓘ Use the Active Directory Domain Services Installation Wizard (dcpromo.exe) to make the server a fully functional domain controller.

Close this wizard and launch the Active Directory Domain Services Installation Wizard (dcpromo.exe).

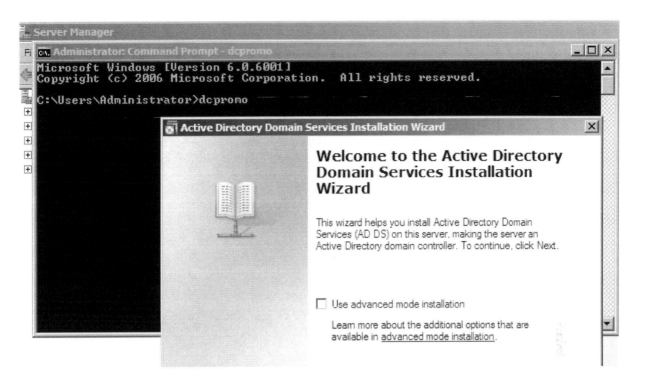

You need to have an NTFS partition with enough free space to hold the AD database files including the Active Directory database, the log files, and the SYSVOL shared folder. These are considered as System State data. For a simple installation with a single hard disk, you may accept the default directories. If you have multiple disks, you want to consider how you may backup the data. Keep in mind, you cannot backup data onto the same disk!

You need a properly functioning network card with proper IP addressing defined. Very importantly, you should use static IP address on this server. DHCP is not recommended. You also need to have an operational DNS server and a domain name for your organization. Without an existing DNS you will need to setup DNS on this same server.

Dcpromo will call up the wizard. You can choose to either join an existing forest or create a new forest. For demonstration purpose we create a new forest here. As the first server it must also act as a global catalog server. DNS should also be installed here. If no existing DNS infrastructure is in place, delegation will not be initially possible.

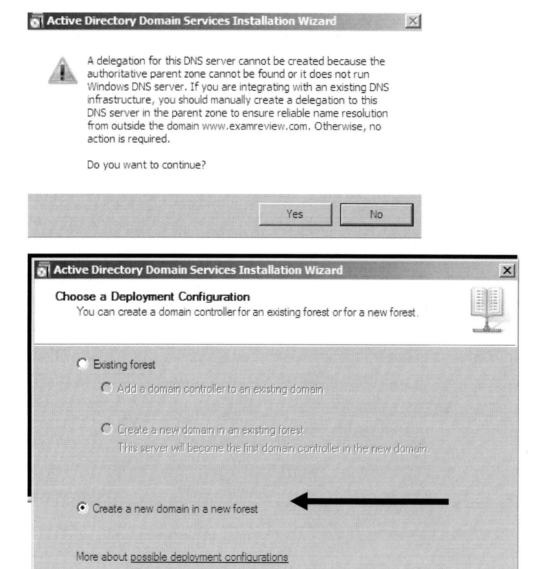

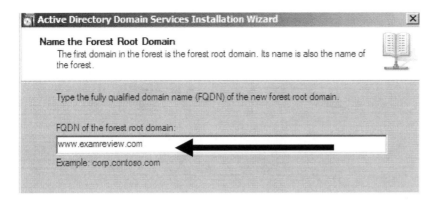

If you install a new Server 2008 R2 domain controller in an existing 2000 Server or Server 2003 based domain, and if this domain controller is also the first Windows Server 2008 R2 domain controller in the forest, you must prepare the forest by extending the schema via adprep. In Windows Server 2008 R2, Adprep.exe can be found in the /support/adprep folder of the DVD disc.

When the first Windows Server 2008–based Domain Controller is introduced, the forest will operate by default at the lowest functional level that is possible, which is Windows 2000, so that you may take advantage of the default Active Directory features while accommodating older versions of Windows Server. If you raise the functional level, newer advanced features can become available at the expense of compatibility. After you raise the domain functional level, domain controllers running earlier operating systems will not be able to participate in the domain. Ask yourself this question - is there a reason why older domain controllers should be retained? You need to be very careful because raising the domain functional levels to Windows Server 2008 is a task that can never be undone. In fact, all the existing Windows 2000–based or Windows Server 2003–based Domain Controllers will no longer function as expected.

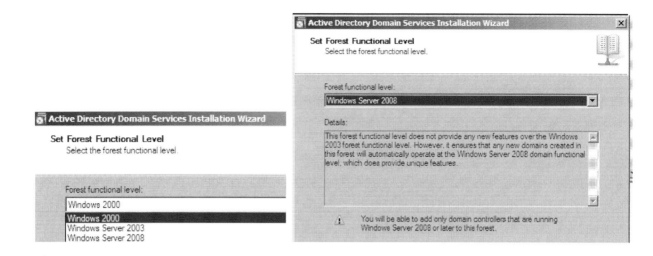

Do keep in mind, you can always raise the functional level later.

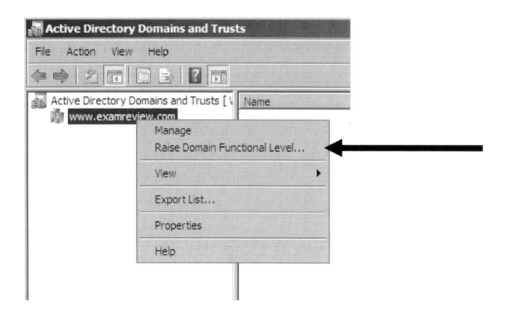

Along the installation process you will be asked to install DNS server. You will be suggested to use static IPs for the server as well.

Additional Domain Controller Options

Select additional options for this domain controller.

☑ DNS server

☑ Global catalog

☐ Read-only domain controller (RODC)

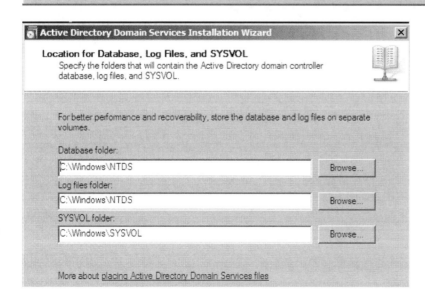

Static IP assignment

This computer has dynamically assigned IP address(es)

This computer has at least one physical network adapter that does not have static IP address(es) assigned to its IP Properties. You should assign static IP address(es) to all physical network adapters for reliable Domain Name System (DNS) operation, for both IPv4 and IPv6 when available. See Help for more information.

Do you want to continue without assigning static IP address(es)?

→ **Yes, the computer will use a dynamically assigned IP address (not recommended).**

→ **No, I will assign static IP addresses to all physical network adapters.**

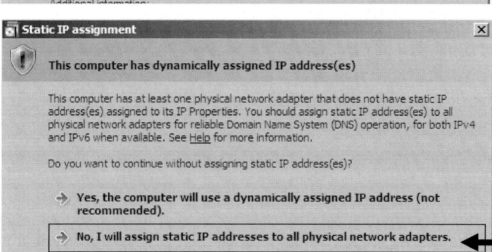

Location for Database, Log Files, and SYSVOL
Specify the folders that will contain the Active Directory domain controller database, log files, and SYSVOL.

For better performance and recoverability, store the database and log files on separate volumes.

Database folder:
C:\Windows\NTDS   Browse...

Log files folder:
C:\Windows\NTDS   Browse...

SYSVOL folder:
C:\Windows\SYSVOL   Browse...

More about placing Active Directory Domain Services files

Directory Services Restore Mode DSRM is an alternate boot environment. With it your Windows Server can boot with the Active Directory database offline so you may perform routine maintenance as needed. Before you may boot into DSRM, the DSRM password must be set. After installation is completed, the server needs to be restarted in order for the new AD consoles to show up.

Active Directory Domain Services Installation Wizard ☒

Directory Services Restore Mode Administrator Password

The Directory Services Restore Mode Administrator account is different from the domain Administrator account.

Assign a password for the Administrator account that will be used when this domain controller is started in Directory Services Restore Mode. We recommend that you choose a strong password.

Password: ●●●●●●●●●●●●●●

Confirm password: ●●●●●●●●●●●●●●

More about Directory Services Restore Mode password

Active Directory Domain Services Installation Wizard ☒

Completing the Active Directory Domain Services Installation Wizard

Active Directory Domain Services is now installed on this computer for the domain www.examreview.com.

This Active Directory domain controller is assigned to the site Default-First-Site-Name. You can manage sites with the Active Directory Sites and Services administrative tool.

To close this wizard, click Finish.

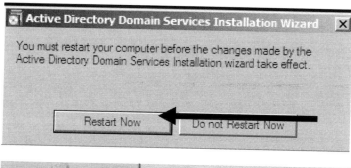

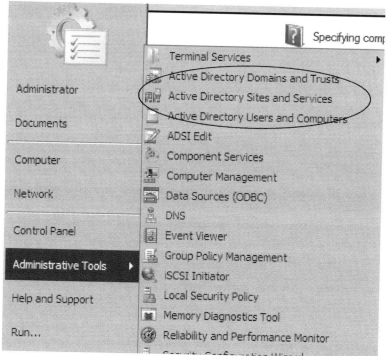

You may use Nltest.exe at the command line to show information on the Active Directory Domain Services. In the future, if you want to remove AD from the server, simply use DCPROMO to call up the wizard again. You will be able to delete AD from there.

Active Directory Domain Services Installation Wizard ☒

Welcome to the Active Directory Domain Services Installation Wizard

This computer is already an Active Directory domain controller. You can use this wizard to uninstall Active Directory Domain Services on this server.

Delete the Domain

Indicate whether this is the last domain controller in the domain.

☐ Delete the domain because this server is the last domain controller in the domain

⚠ The domain will no longer exist after you uninstall Active Directory Domain Services from the last domain controller in the domain. Before you continue:

Be aware that all user and computer accounts will be deleted.

Be aware that all computers that belong to this domain will not be able to log on to the domain or access domain services anymore.

All cryptographic keys will be deleted. We recommend that you export them before proceeding.

Decrypt all encrypted data such as Encrypting File System (EFS)-encrypted files or e-mail before deleting the domain; otherwise, this data will be permanently inaccessible.

Active Directory Domain Services Installation Wizard ☒

Confirm Deletion
Removing Active Directory Domain Services will delete all application partitions from this Active Directory domain controller.

Confirm that you want the wizard to delete all application directory partitions on this Active Directory domain controller. The partitions will be deleted when the wizard is completed.

☐ Delete all application directory partitions on this Active Directory domain controller.

⚠ Deleting the last replica of an application partition deletes all data associated with that partition.

Roles and Operation Masters

Updating Active Directory objects can usually be performed by any domain controller unless the domain controller is read-only. After an object is updated on one, the changes will be propagated to all other domain controllers through replication. HOWEVER, some types of updates must be handled by specific Domain Controllers known as Flexible Single Master Operations FSMO roles, including

- Schema Master

- Domain Naming Master

- Infrastructure Master

- Relative ID RID Master

- Primary Domain Controller PDC Emulator

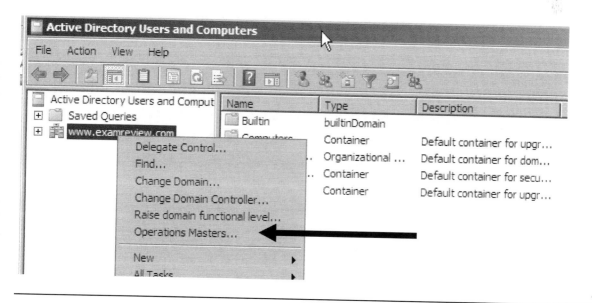

You want to know that all schema changes are processed by the Schema Master. This role is always kept in the forest root domain, and that you should place it on the same domain controller as the PDC emulator, which is the authoritative domain controller in a domain and the default domain controller for most administrative tools. In fact this PDC emulator also serves as the authoritative time source.

When domains join or leave a forest, the domain naming master makes the updates and commits the necessary changes into AD. You want this role to be performed by the PDC emulator of the forest root. Each domain needs to have its very own infrastructure master, which performs name translation between globally unique identifiers (GUIDs), security identifiers (SIDs), and distinguished names (DNs) for all foreign domain objects. Each domain also needs to have a domain controller with the RID master role to handling relative IDs arrangement. You want to have this role assigned to a domain controller that also serves as a PDC emulator.

Generally, schema master and domain naming master are assigned once in the domain at the forest root only. RID master, PCD emulator, and Infrastructure Master, on the other hand, are assigned in each domain to the same domain controller in there. A standby operations master is one which can assume the operations master role should the original computer fails. One domain controller can act as the standby operations master for all operations master roles within a domain, and of course you can have more.

A RODC Read Only DC is simply an additional domain controller that hosts read-only partitions of the Active Directory database. It is primarily for use in branch office with poor WAN link. RODC can keep cached credentials so faster login can be made possible.

You want to know that the first domain controller in a forest must NOT be an RODC. Also keep in mind, before you may install any RODC in a Windows 2000 Server or Windows Server 2003 forest, you must first prepare the forest using adprep /rodcprep. As previously said, in Windows Server 2008 R2 Adprep.exe can be found in the /support/adprep folder of the DVD disc.

Questions:

1. What command can you use to invoke the AD Installation Wizard?

2. How do you run the AD Installation Wizard in advanced mode?

3. AD database files include:

4. You may prepare a forest by extending the schema via what tool?

5. In Windows Server 2008 R2, Adprep.exe can be found in which location?

6. When the first Windows Server 2008–based Domain Controller is introduced, the forest will operate by default at the _____ functional level that is possible.

Answers:

1. *You need to use the dcpromo command to invoke the AD Installation Wizard.*

2. *If you use the /adv switch you can run the wizard in advanced mode.*

3. *You need to have an NTFS partition with enough free space to hold the AD database files including the Active Directory database, the log files, and the SYSVOL shared folder. These are considered as System State data.*

4. *If you install a new Server 2008 R2 domain controller in an existing 2000 Server or Server 2003 based domain, and if this domain controller is also the first Windows Server 2008 R2 domain controller in the forest, you must prepare the forest by extending the schema via adprep.*

5. *In Windows Server 2008 R2, Adprep.exe can be found in the /support/adprep folder of the DVD disc.*

6. *When the first Windows Server 2008–based Domain Controller is introduced, the forest will operate by default at the lowest functional level that is possible, which is Windows 2000.*

End of book

Made in the USA
Charleston, SC
14 November 2016

About ExamREVIEW.NET

ExamREVIEW is an independent content developer not associated/affiliated with the certification vendor(s) mentioned throughout this book. The name(s), title(s) and award(s) of the certification exam(s) mentioned in this book are the trademark(s) of the respective certification vendor(s). We mention these name(s) and/or the relevant terminologies only for describing the relevant exam process(es) and knowledge. We at ExamREVIEW develop study material entirely on our own without endorsement from the certification vendor(s). Our material is fully copyrighted. Braindump is strictly prohibited. We provide essential knowledge contents, NOT any generalized "study system" kind of "pick-the-right-answer-every time" techniques or "visit this link" referrals. We keep prices low by eliminating all the non-essential study features.

We are NOT affiliated with Microsoft. This book is also NOT endorsed by Microsoft. The MTA exams are the property of Microsoft.

EXAMREVIEW.NET
NO FRILLS Exam Prep Books

ISBN 9781508416012
9000

9 781508 416012